(Foundation Report No. 3.)

Solar and Lunar Returns

HOW THEY AFFECT YOU

According to the Sidereal Zodiac

Including a Complete Ephemeris
of the
VERNAL POINT
1849 to 1960

By DONALD A. BRADLEY
Research Director
The Llewellyn Foundation for Astrological Research

Llewellyn Publications
Box 3383
St. Paul, Minn. 55165

All rights reserved. No part of this book, neither in part nor in whole, may be reproduced, transmitted or utilized in any form or by any means, electronic or mechanical, including photocopying, recording, or by any information storage and retrieval system, without permission in writing from the Publisher, except for brief quotations embodied in critical articles and reviews.

Original publication 1948
Second impression 1968
Third impression 1973
Fourth impression 1974

Publisher: LLEWELLYN PUBLICATIONS, St. Paul, Minn. U.S.A.
Typographer: Llewellyn Publications, Ltd., Los Angeles, Calif. U.S.A.

FOREWORD

"To stop short in any research that bids fair to widen the gates of knowledge, to recoil from fear of difficulty or adverse criticism, is to bring reproach upon science." —Sir William Crooks

 WAS never so forcibly compelled to realize the truth of the foregoing quotation from one of the world's greatest scientists as when the astonishing findings of research on the Sidereal Zodiac were brought before me for study.

With this poignant admonition of Sir William Crooks in mind, I set out sturdily, come what may in the way of mental jolts, to make an unbiased study of the Sidereal Zodiac system of making and delineating Solunar Returns.

Long ago I discontinued using the conventional "standard" system of Solar and Lunar Returns because their indices were usually unsatisfactory. Nevertheless, a belief remained that "there was gold in those fields" and this hope enhanced the urge to investigate. Sure enough, "gold" was found in this modern revival of successful ancient practice which involves the Sidereal Zodiac of the Constellations.

One of the faults of the conventional Tropical Zodiac Return Chart is that as one grows older an error accumulates so that at middle age the error can be as much as eighteen hours, due to the continual shifting of the Vernal Point at the rate of fifty seconds of longitude yearly; and this cannot properly be adjusted by deductions from the Sun's position, as explained by Cyril Fagan under the heading, "The Solar Returns of Egypt and Babylon," in the Astrological Bulletina Annual, issue No. 254; and amplified in his striking book, "Zodiacs Old and New."

Donald A. Bradley, author of this important book on "Solar and Lunar Returns," treated through the Sidereal Zodiac, is a deep, careful researcher, possessing the rare gift of keen insight with which to evaluate research findings, and make accurate deductions with capable conveyance of the information to students in clear, understandable language.

The author does not compare this new system with the conventional method. He definitely outlines a complete, practical application that is a wide departure from the beaten path, as it employs new rules and new terms which represent an advance in the understanding and application of this branch of astrology through evaluation of the ancient and original system of casting Solar and Lunar Return Charts.

Therefore, by approaching this study of Solunar Returns with an unprejudiced and open mind, those who like to explore new ways to better technique, will be amply rewarded. Herein a vast, rich frontier of study has been opened to something really promising for those who dare to enter it.

Because the system **works**—however strange some of its postulates may seem to those who are versed only in the orthodox method, and because so many inquiring students desire to learn **how** it works—this book is designed to open for them new, broad vistas. It guides those who would venture from the beaten path into new fields of exploration for the purpose of acquiring simpler techniques for greater accuracy in predictive science.

Thirty-one charts illustrate the text: fascinating studies toward a liberal education in this phase of astrology.

So we wend our way into the Constellations to discover the reason and method by which great astrologers of ancient times were enabled to make their famous and far-reaching predictions.

—Llewellyn George

SOLAR AND LUNAR RETURNS
How They Affect You

—— **Contents** ——

Chapter 1:

    REINSTATING THE CLASSICAL ZODIAC   9 to 17

    Better Work With Better Tools, 9. Relationship of the Two Zodiacs, 11. Solunar Returns, 12. The "Grain" of Solunar Charts, 13. Secondary Return Charts, 15. An Astrological Pitfall, 16.

Chapter 2:

    HOW TO CAST SOLUNAR RETURN CHARTS . 18 to 27

    The Vernal Point Ephemeris, 18. Converting to the Sidereal Zodiac, 18. Finding the Sun's Longitude, 19. A Complete Working Example, 20. Table of General Precession, 23.

Chapter 3:

    SOLUNAR INTERPRETATION: THE SUN . 28 to 40

    The Sun in the Foreground, 28. The Sun in the Middleground, 30. The Sun in the Background, 32. Solar Aspects, 32.

Chapter 4:

    SOLUNAR INTERPRETATION: THE MOON . 41 to 46

    The Moon in the Foreground, 41. The Moon in the Middleground, 42. The Moon in the Background, 42. Lunar Aspects, 43.

Chapter 5:

    SOLUNAR INTERPRETATION: THE PLANETS, 47 to 56

    Mercury, 47. Venus, 49. Mars, 51. Jupiter, 53. Saturn, 54. Uranus, 55. Neptune, 56. Pluto, 56.

Chapter 6:

    SOLUNAR RETURNS IN ACTION . . . . 57 to 82

    The Bitter and the Sweet, 58. The Great, 61. And the Small, 62. Death Sentence, 65. The Winnah!, 67. Farewell to a Friend, 72. Those Fell Clutches, 73. He Let George Do It, 75. Go Right to the Source for Your Information, 77. Mooney's Moon, 77. A Royal Flush, 80. More Than Mayhem in Mexico, 81.

Chapter 7:
 CRISES IN CONSCIOUSNESS . . . . . . 83 to 87
 Don't Belittle Locality Charts, 85.

AUXILIARY TABLE Showing Amounts of General Precession
 for Intervals of Years 23

EPHEMERIS OF THE VERNAL POINT,
 1849—1960 . . . . 88 to 115

HOW TO DETERMINE CAMPANIAN HOUSE CUSPS
 using a Standard Placidian Table of Houses . . . 116—117

ILLUSTRATIONS . . . . 122—123

TABLES OF CUSP TRANSPOSITIONS . . . 118 to 121

CHAPTER 1

REINSTATING THE CLASSICAL ZODIAC

Better Work With Better Tools

SEVERAL HUNDRED PEOPLE may die instantly during the detonation of a bomb or explosion of a munitions-laden vessel. Are we to believe that the progressed chart of each and every one of the victims is so severely "afflicted" at the time of the catastrophe that Fate in some strange way arranges and directs their movements so cleverly that a particular event is destined to be a common doomsday? A volcano may explode and snuff out 30,000 lives in one blinding, hellish roar. An astrological explanation of the tectonic eruption is easy, in terms of eclipses, ingresses, and even comets; not to mention hypothetical planets and "critical points" probably extant only in imagination. Viewing the whole problem impartially, we astrologers must admit that the challenge it presents is disconcerting, to say the least, unless we have long overlooked techniques and tools which account for such unusually effective pranks of nature, blasphemously called "acts of God."

The progressed horoscope can hardly be blamed for all, or even any, for that matter, of these cataclysmic happenings which affect, harm or destroy human lives. Opponents of astrology point out this problem as a breach, a gaping loophole in our conceptual scheme of things. They bray and bellow their (somewhat justified) criticism that we are presumptuous enough to account for a common cold, but often fail to foresee major disasters. We have to admit, albeit not sheepishly, that astrology, like all other departments of scientific thought, is still in its infancy. Although the oldest, indeed, the very matrix, of all sciences, it is still in the toe-counting, toddling stage. One answer, on the evasive side, perhaps, but fairly given to our challengers, is that we are not presumptuous enough to believe that we "know it all." We do know that planetary influences are a reality. The exact how and wherefore does not greatly bother us at the moment, and rightly so. This old world of ours would have been rather dark for countless eons if the gods had awaited man's discovery of photons before allowing us sunshine and starlight or even flint. We know that the duodenary division of the apparent celestial sphere into sectors which qualify planetary influences is a reality. Some day we will find out just how planetary, zodiacal and domal influences are possible, but these are riddles the solutions to which we bequest to future generations of inquirers.

Astrologers today are working hard in behalf of the future when they will have won the recognition and plaudits they deserve for keeping astrology alive and awake during its three-century-long exile from institutions of "higher learning" (!). However, the time is now long overdue when astrologers should begin to question the adequacy of their colorful tradition to account for all the vicissitudes and ecstasies of modern life. All other sciences, as time passes, undergo broad metamorphoses with the new additions and discoveries which enhance them over the years. What is held to be superior in one decade is revised or discarded the next in favor of another view or method. Zigzagging is rightfully encouraged, so long as it is a forward motion, however oblique. Improvements, revisions, fearless criticisms, and bold suggestions are welcome in all the academic provinces of learning. Yet, astrology's paraphernalia remains to a great extent as it was in previous generations. Its techniques and meanings continue as naive or complex, as the case may be, as they were in Sibly's or Lilly's day. This, to one way of thinking, is a tender virtue of our science. From a progressive standpoint, this stereotype is anything but creditable, for it represents a crystallization of talent.

There are several hundred "qualified" astrologers in the United States today, which alone implies an over-ripeness of the field for genuine, basic innovations. The situation reminds the outsider of the record of Christian missionary achievements in Siam during the past half-century. Several hundred missionaries, representing many various denominations, have labored in that Eastern field so white unto harvest with the net result being about ten thousand conversions to Christianity. The population of Siam is around fifteen million.

Contrary to current opinion in our field, astrology's future improvements will not tend toward mathematical refinement alone. Too many of us have wangled our ways through the fascinating jungle of figures and formulas, only to return almost empty-handed of anything truly worthwhile, aside from a realization that much valuable time has been wasted. The greatest further development of astrology is in the region of interpretation and application, as stressed by Llewellyn George (in the fourth chapter of his "Lectures on Astrology"). This is not conjectural, for we already have learned, since only 1944, that a vast, rich frontier of study has been opened up to us in the way of something really promising. Those of us who have scouted the fringes of this frontier can assure our colleagues that great rewards are in store for anyone who bravely sets forth to explore this new vista. This "lost horizon," found anew in our modern age of wires and windows and wheels, is the **classical zodiac** of antiquity. This zodiac, differing markedly from the "zodiac" we customarily work and think with, is that of the twelve **constellations** which bear the same names we have retained for the **signs**. The practical application of this constellation or **sidereal zodiac,** in the form of special **predictive** techniques, is a new plane of thought in modern astrology. These predictive techniques excel in accuracy and lucidity any method of prognosis heretofore advanced in our subject. This is a mighty big claim, but its backing is mighty persuasive, too. So overwhelmingly convincing is the worth of the method, even in its first try-outs, that the newcomer is invariably astonished at the fact that it has taken so long to come to light.

The historic and scientific proof of the validity of the sidereal zodiac has been fully covered in recently released publications, so it is superfluous to repeat at length any of this data. Statistical research completely confirms the reality of the sidereal zodiac, while the proof is undeniable that the astrologers of ancient times used it exclusively, unmindful of the present-day system of marking off the zodiacal divisions. As pointed out by several authorities, the reinstatement of the classical zodiac of the starry constellations in no merciless way invalidates the "standard" **tropical zodiac** which has been in common use for centuries throughout the Western world. (Oriental astrology has always been based upon a constellational zodiac; we Westerners have respected this fact, although seldom have we suspected its true worth.) Argumentation avails little; the proof of the pudding is in the eating. Protests by the uninformed or misinformed, that the introduction of the sidereal zodiac is too drastic a departure from standardized ways and means, are hardly worth heeding, considering their source. Sidereal astrology **works,** and that is sufficient justification, by any criterion, for its adoption.

Relationship of the Two Zodiacs

In its ceaseless motion through space and time, the earth is subject to numerous effects, due to the by-play and back-play of the gravitational attraction of other bodies, which alter its otherwise fixed orbit and inclination. The chief result of this interchange of effects is called **precession of the equinoxes.** More correctly, the motion is one of **recession,** for it is a slow westward (clockwise) movement of the equinoxes against the broad, star-studded backdrop of the celestial sphere. The equinoxes are the points of intersection of the ecliptic and the equator. The Vernal Equinox is the point where the Sun, always moving on the ecliptic, cuts across the equator in moving from the southern hemisphere to the northern. This annual passage occurs on or about March 21st every year and marks the beginning of the Spring season for us who live in the northern hemisphere. The Autumnal Equinox is the point just opposite in the sky to the Vernal where the Sun crosses the equator to again enter the southern hemisphere. As intimated by its name, the occurrence designates the beginning of the Autumn season. This situation is elementary astronomy, familiar to every modern schoolboy and girl.

Now, in standardized astrological practice, the twelve "signs of the zodiac" are counted from the Vernal Point, with each "sign" permanently allotted successive thirty-degree segments of the whole circle of the ecliptic, irrespective of the stars. The sign Aries is held to commence at 0° of celestial longitude (also called geocentric longitude), or, in other words, at the Vernal Point. The span of the sign

Aries is the first thirty-degree arc measured from this fixed point. Taurus follows, taking up the next one-twelfth of the great circle, etc. Because the twelve signs, Aries, Taurus, Gemini, Cancer, Leo, and so on, are fixed with reference to this Vernal Point, they are **in motion** because the Vernal Point itself is in motion under the stress of the several forces which together constitute precession.

This state of affairs clearly in mind, it is now understandable why the **signs** of the zodiac no longer correspond to the zodiacal **constellations** which are their original namesakes. Hence, the **sign** of Aries is now in the **constellation** of Pisces, for if Aries in modern astrological usage starts at the Vernal Point, and that point now lies far from the starfield of the Ram and in the asterism of the Fishes, a superimposition is inevitable. In like manner, due to the constant westward slippage of the Vernal Point (which makes a complete circuit of the heavens in about 25,000 years), all the signs of the zodiac are now nearly "one remove" from the constellations after which they were named two thousand years ago. The "moving zodiac" (tropical) and the "fixed zodiac" (sidereal) exactly coincided in 213 A. D., as determined by Mr. Cyril Fagan, the re-discoverer of the classical system. The whole astrological world is indebted to Mr. Fagan of Dublin, Ireland, for the superb achievement which his discoveries and contributions represent. The reader has an intellectual treat in store in the published writings of this authority on the astrology of antiquity.

Solunar Returns

Inasmuch as **"solar returns"** and **"lunar returns,"** as referred entirely to the sidereal zodiac, were the primary working tools of ancient astrologers, we are behooved to investigate the value of these old methods long forgotten by astrological students of the present age. Frequent mention of **"solunar returns"** in ancient astrological texts incited a few modern students to try their hand at the technique. But, alas, not knowing that this technique is workable only in terms of the constellational zodiac, only discouragement and embarassment resulted. Two or three more courageous astrologers even went so far as to write texts on "solar revolutions," but it is admitted by leaders throughout the astrological fraternity that "solar revolutions," based upon the tropical (standard) zodiac, are usually failures. Hence, the use of these erroneous solar returns was mostly abandoned in favor of the more sound methods of chart-progression. Every now and then, over the years, a valiant student will attempt a resuscitation of the method, but, simply because of its failure, such a method has never become popular with the rank and file of careful astrologicoes.

However, with the rediscovery of the zodiac of antiquity, together with fuller and more comprehensive translations of archaic texts, we now know the correct way to cast and read solunar return charts.

A SOLAR RETURN chart is cast for the time the Sun occupies the exact point with reference to the fixed stars that it held in the birthchart.

This occurs one moment out of every sidereal year, around the calendar date of the anniversary of birth. Such a chart, cast for the native's place of residence, is a life-chart for the year which follows and terminates with the return of the Sun to that vital spot once again. A solar return chart describes, by the aspects and positions of the planets, the events to befall the native during the ensuing twelve months, the "vibratory" conditions under which he will live and move and have his being, and, generally, the "accidents" slated to affect him physically and morally.

The LUNAR RETURN chart is cast for the time when the Moon occupies the exact point with reference to the fixed stars that it held in the birthchart.

Because the Moon makes this "return" every 27.3 days, or thereabouts, the influence of the lunar return prevails over the 27 days subsequent to the phenomenon. Basically a **health** chart, the lunar return has a direct impact upon the physical and nervous well-being of the native, although its importance does not end there. The lunar return is decidedly more critical in its effects than the less concentrated solar return, and is found to foreshadow the major happenings in the native's life during the **month** in question. The approach to all solunar interpretation is made as though the chart were a **natus** of the native.

The "Grain" of Solunar Charts

Considerable differences from the customary approach toward delineating "standard" horoscopes exist where solunar returns are concerned. The student must bear these divergencies from habit in mind at all times until he is thoroughly conditioned to the new plane of thinking to which he has elevated himself. First of all, it is not allowable to think in terms of **"house rulerships."** The chart is used exclusively in the context of the constellations, thereby voiding any such attempt to use the familiar trick of house rulerships to arrive at a conclusion. Such a ruling as this is certainly welcome, as it greatly simplifies the reading of indications. The natures of the planets are innate and inflexible. Use of the "lords" and "ladies" of the various constellations, as well as their "dignities and debilities," is permissible, but **not as disposers** in the chart.

Another difference from "standard" practice lies in the assessment of the relative power and importance of the planets in solunar charts. This is determined by their house positions. The **angular houses** (1st, 4th, 7th and 10th) constitute what is known as **"the foreground"** of any chart. Planets in angular houses, or within orb of conjunction of the horizon or meridian, are said to be "in the foreground," where they are at maximum opportunity to help or hurt, to bless or blight.

The **succedent houses** (2nd, 5th, 8th and 11th) make up what is known as **"the middleground"** of the chart. Planets here are of secondary importance. The four **cadent houses** (3rd, 6th, 9th and 12th), comprising **"the background,"** are of least important, for in them the planets are shorn of their power for actuating any great good or adversity. (From the standpoint of health, the Luminaries in the foreground are splendid vitalizers, but in the background, bodily resistance and restorative powers are lowered along with the general vitality.)

A third difference rests in the interpretation of aspects. Inasmuch as the "planetary natures" are held to be inviolably fixed, their inherent influences are not in any way qualified by the "nature" of the aspect. Conjunctions, oppositions and squares are the most important aspects, followed by the less abrupt and less coercive trines and sextiles. In all application of solunar techniques, **only the five major aspects** are taken into consideration. The natures of the planets involved determine the meaning of the configuration, and not the popularly assumed "nature" of the aspect concerned. In other words, **any** aspect involving Mars, Saturn or Neptune, trines and sextiles included, is read as an adverse indication. Any aspect between the Luminaries and Venus, Jupiter or Uranus, squares and oppositions included, are taken as favorable auguries. The truth of this will descend with an impact upon the newcomer conditioned to thinking "all squares are bad and all trines are good, etc."

Fourth: All transits are referred to **the nativity equated to the locality** rather than to the birthplace, unless no change of residence or position has taken place. The "reading" of the birthchart, of course, remains indelible, but, so far as transits of the planets are concerned, the cusps of the locality-chart houses are those used to evaluate the effects of transitive indications. It is a simple matter to make this equation: Find the difference in geographic longitude between the birthplace and the present locality of the native. If the new locality is **east** of the birthplace, **add** this amount (either in time or arc, as preferred) to the R. A. M. C. or Sidereal Time of the original birthchart. The sum is the correct R. A. M. C. or Sidereal Time of the locality chart. If the new locality is **west** of the birthplace, **subtract** this amount from the radix R. A. M. C. or S. T., and the result is the S. T. of the locality chart. Then enter the table of houses for the latitude of the locality, and extract therefrom the appropriate cusps. The planetary longitudes are unchanged in this shift, although their mundane (house) positions will change accordingly.

A fifth, no less important, departure from the usual mechanics of chart construction and use lies in the controversy-ridden matter of domification (house-division). There can be little doubt but what the Campanian system of houses is far superior to the Placidian now in almost universal use. No complete or even nearly-complete table of Campanian cusps has yet been printed, and so is unavailable on the astrological market. Until this sorry shortcoming is remedied (as will happen in the near future, we know), students will have to be content with the tables of houses now in their possession, when working with latitudes for which Campanian cusps have not been published. However, a slight calculation to each cusp will adjust them (except Midheaven and Ascendant) to the Campanian figures. See **Contents** for section on "How to Determine the Campanian House Cusps."

To be absolutely in keeping with the requirements of sidereal techniques, Campanian cusps are a necessity, and should be used whenever possible. The truth of this will also glare forth to anyone who will experiment with the problem. The whole foreground-middleground-background scheme rests solidly upon the natural division of the apparent celestial sphere afforded by the Campanus system, and that alone.

Aside from the immediately foregoing matter, it will now be clear to the reader that the delineation of solunar charts is immensely simpler than perhaps previously supposed. The very simplicity of the solunar technique is one of its prize advantages and wonder-working attributes. We must now face the less agreeable responsibility of learning to "convert zodiacs" and erect solunar return charts.

Secondary Return Charts

The return of the Sun to a conjunction of its natal place in the stellar zodiac holds good, in its inferences, for the full year running until its next return to the same point. The Moon's return to its radical point is fully effective until its passage completely around the zodiac brings it back again to that same crucial spot, a matter of about four weeks. But it has been discovered by active researchers that "returns" of the Sun and Moon to **opposition** and **square** of their radical positions also wield some appreciable influence in the life. These have been referred to as **demi-solar** and **demi-lunar returns**, although such terms are appropriate only for the "opposition charts." The "square charts" may conveniently be distinguished by use of the terms **quarti-solar** and **quarti-lunar returns**.

This new development in the theory and practice of solunar techniques lends an unexpected note of complexity to the whole subject, but fortunately affords the astrologer with a **timing tool** by which he may "pin down" on the calendar the **week within a month** during which the fulfillment of a monthly indication is most likely to take place. Events discernible in a lunar return may, potentially, materialize any time during the four weeks covered by the chart.

Actually, however, these events will become realities in the week covered by a quarti-lunar chart showing similar potentialities. Hence, should the monthly chart show a propitious Jupiterian boon, it may safely be assumed that the most probable time for this influence to manifest itself fully is during the 6- or 7-day period when Jupiter again is highly auspicious.

The first week following a lunar return (proper) will experience an unmodified playing-forth of the influences. However, when the Moon reaches the dexter square of its own place, a chart struck for this time has a qualifying tendency over the original conjunction-chart. Likewise with the third and fourth weeks of the sidereal month.

And likewise, too, with the functioning of the four 3-month periods in a sidereal year. The solar return chart (proper) can be terminologically identified as the **Solar Return**, the **Annual Chart**, the **Yearly Chart**, etc. Solar returns to square angles with its radical place may be called **Quarterly Charts**. The demi-solar return, which is effective for the last half of the year, is called the **Semester Chart**. Easy terms for the corresponding types of lunar charts are: **Monthly, Sennight,** and **Fortnight Charts,** in the immediate absence of more fitting designations. "Sennight" is an old word meaning "a week," and "fortnight" refers to a two-week period; hence their choice.

It has not seemed necessary, to the writer, at least, to set up every demi- and quarti-solunar return figure, for the simple professional or general application of astrology. Nothing in outright contradiction to the monthly or yearly return chart is likely, despite the modifying or amplifying tendencies of the secondary charts. The astrological student, nevertheless, apart from professional or general activities, would be wise to take the extra time and trouble of computing **all** his demi- and quarti-return figures, for the light they will shed on the details of daily living. **Astrology must be lived to be learned!**

An Astrological Pitfall

There are ten transiting planets, and ten radical planets. There are five "Ptolemaic" or major aspects which transiting bodies can make with radix planets: the conjunction, sextile, square, trine, and opposition. This, then, technically allows eight major aspects to occur between ten transitive and ten natal planets, which further means that, excluding even the Ascendant and Midheaven points, there are **eighty** vital points in the horoscope of birth which can be "touched off" by any of ten transiting planets! Little wonder is it, therefore, that a superficially trained astrological practitioner can find "indices" of **anything** that ever happens to an individual by comparing transits with the birthchart! It may astonish the newer student to learn that **the odds are even that at any given moment a transiting** planet is within 0°27' of a conjunction, square or opposition, of a natal planet—a fact which gives the lie to many current astrological (mal)practices.

This fact is brought to the reader's attention so that he will appreciate more fully the writer's insistence that astrology as a whole, is a science, not a game, and that it is folly to "explain" a misfortune, for example, by merely listing what appears to be an impressive series of "bad aspects" simultaneously operating in the horoscope. The tabulated transits must be **appropriate to the eventuality**; the mere presence of squares and oppositions, by themselves considered, have little weight as an explanation. The shedding of blood because of a pierced epidermis is due to Mars' action, and not to any other planet. Similarly, the destruction of tissue, as through bruises, is due to Saturnian influence, and to list other, wholly diverse planetary influences as the cause, is to make blatant misuse of the simplest astrological tenets. Since the likelihood is so great that so-called "adverse influences" may be found at work at any random moment, it is advisable that the novice-student restrict his studies and observations to only the major aspects during a considerable part of his education, until he has become fully cognizant of such mental pitfalls as this one we have pointed out.

CHAPTER 2

HOW TO CAST SOLUNAR RETURN CHARTS

The Vernal Point Ephemeris

IN THE ABSENCE of ephemerides which give the planets' daily position in sidereal longitude for years back, the user of solunar techniques must himself make the transformations from one zodiac to the other. This is an easy matter, so long as the exact position of the **Vernal Point** is known for the date in question. The Vernal Point, abbreviated "VP," remember, is what is commonly known as "the first point of Aries" (meaning, of course, the tropical sign Aries). Presently, it is about 24° west of the first degree of the constellation Aries, the Ram, or about 6° of the constellation Pisces. Its exact longitude in the constellation Pisces is found in the **VP ephemeris** printed in the back part of this volume. There you will find the correct position given every 10 days from 1849 to 1960, inclusive. Inspection of the VP ephemeris will show what extremes of wobbling the VP undergoes in the course of a year, under the impetus of the combined forces of precession and nutation. Calculation of this massive table was far more tedious and complicated than might be supposed by any layman unacquainted with the intricacies of astronomical computation. The author and his publisher are proud to make it available, for its great practical value as well as for the mathematical achievement its production represents.

The first-magnitude star **Spica** is the "fiducial" or constant determinator of the measurement of sidereal longitude, for that important star (Alpha Virginis) was believed by the ancients of Chaldea, Egypt, India and China, to mark exactly 29°00′ of the constellation Virgo. The position of Spica, therefore, is used as the basis for all sidereal-zodiac (abbreviated "SZ") calculations. The Vernal Point which is 0° Aries of the tropical zodiac (abbreviated "TZ") recedes a full degree every 72 years, at the rate of about 50″ per annum. It is absoultely necessary to have the sidereal longitude of the VP to the exact degree, minute and second, when computing solar returns. Lunar returns require only the correct degree and minute.

Converting to the Sidereal Zodiac

At Greenwich Mean Noon (= Noon Mark anywhere) on January 1st, 1850, the Sun's tropical longitude was 10°47′49″ Capricorn, according to every accepted astrological ephemeris.

Consulting the first page of the VP ephemeris (see index), you will learn that the sidereal longitude of that marking-point is 7°15′16″ Pisces. This is 22°44′44″ west of 0° of the constellation Aries, so this amount must be **subtracted** from the tropical longitude of the Sun to obtain its correct sidereal longitude. Hence,

```
    Sun   10°47'49"  Capricorn (the sign).
  minus   22 44 44
  gives   18 03 05   Sagittarius (the constellation).
```

It is much easier to make direct use of the VP's given longitude to make this conversion of zodiacs. You do this by **adding** the given value of degree, minutes and seconds (ignoring its position in Pisces) to the tropical longitude, and then subtracting 30°00'00" from the sum in order to get the correct constellation (by name, that is). Thus,

```
    Sun   10°47'49"  Capricorn (TZ)
   plus    7 15 16   (longitude of VP)
          18 03 05   Capricorn
  minus   30 00 00
  gives   18 03 05   Sagittarius (SZ).
```

Obviously, the step "minus 30°" is wholly superfluous, as the operation in actual practice will be done mentally. The student will quickly become accustomed to thinking in terms of "one sign remove (backward)," whenever he has to make a conversion of zodiacs.

Another example is fitting. On October 8th, 1903, at Noon Mark, the Sun was at 14°01'30" of the sign Libra, while the VP was 6°30'24" Pisces. What was its SZ longitude? Simply

```
     to   14°01'30"  Libra (TZ)
    add    6 30 24   (VP)
          20 31 54
```

and mentally deduct a whole sign which gives 20°31'54" Virgo (SZ).

The Moon on the same day was 6°15' Taurus (TZ).

```
   Moon    6°15'  Taurus (TZ)
   plus    6 30   (VP)
     is   12 45   Aries (SZ).
```

Every planet is treated in this same simple way, as well as the house cusps of a chart which is being converted into constellational terms.

Finding the Sun's Longitude

The most annoying element in the whole procedure is the inescapable necessity that the Sun's natal longitude must be correctly determined to the second of arc. There are several ways of coping with this problem, albeit all ways require more careful effort than any other phase of the calculations. The best way, by far, is to make direct use of a book of simple tables, entitled, **"Tables of Diurnal Planetary Motion,"** published by the National Astrological Library in Washington, D. C.* We suggest that the reader intent upon the

---

* These tables are available through Llewellyn Publications, Ltd.

application of solunar techniques immediately procure a copy of this valuable book, if he has not done so already. While the aforementioned tables afford the greatest ease and accuracy of computing the Sun's radix longitude (as well as positions of all other bodies, for that matter), and for the finding of the time of the solar return, some students may prefer to continue using the **Ternary Proportional Logarithms** found in "Chamber's Seven-Figure Mathematical Tables." Chamber's is a British volume highly useful to the technical student. Alan Leo and his predecessors have publicized the advantages of the use of "TP logs," so their use is widely known.

One well-known astrological teacher advises the use of the arithmetical method of determining the Sun's correct longitude to seconds of arc. This method is one of long-division by using the rule-of-three proportion formula. To us, this seems to be unduly tedious and time-consuming.

One little-known method, as easy if not actually easier than using TP logs, is the method of **Sexagesimal Logarithms.** Those already familiar with their use do not need instructions toward that end, and because we do not recommend their use by the beginner, it is not desirable to sidetrack here to demonstrate.

Since it is apparent, now, that there are several ways of computing the radix Sun's longitude, and the reverse-problem of determining the time of solar return, there is little use in wasting space by giving many examples of the various systems. It is expedient for the student to have a copy of one or more of these tables in his possession and constantly on hand. Because each of these published tables carries its own instructions, together with adequate step-by-step examples, we will accomplish nothing by repetition of this sort.

A Complete Working Example

The master-mind of psychiatry, and founder of the science of psychoanalysis, was Sigmund Freud, whose name is familiar even to the most indifferent yokelry. Let us convert his horoscope from tropical to sidereal terms as a thorough-going example of the way all charts should be dealt with in the absence of a SZ ephemeris for the year of birth, or if the chart under scrutiny is already on hand and needs proper alignment with the classical zodiac.

Sigmund Freud was born at 9:23 A. M., Local Mean Time, on May 6th, 1856, in the small Moravian town of Freiberg, Czechoslovakia. Freiberg's geographic latitude is 49°38′ North; its longitude, in time, is 1h12m32s East of Greenwich. (Freiberg's Noon Mark is therefore 1:12:32 P. M.) Hence, the man destined to cause the greatest scientific revolution, since Darwin, came into this world 21h 23m after Freiberg Mean Noon of May 5th, 1856. (Or 20h 10m 28s after Noon Mark of May 5th.)

The sidereal longitude of the VP for May 6th, 1856, is 7°09′33″ Pisces, according to the ephemeris.

The sidereal time of birth figures out to be 0h20m29s.

The first step, after cusps of houses are extracted from appropriate tables of houses, is to find the Sun's tropical longitude, in the usual way. Never use the familiar Diurnal Proportional Logarithms to do this, as interpolation is both tedious and cumbersome, and errors too frequently creep into the process.

Since the Sun's daily motion is known to be 0°58'03", all that is required at this stage is to find how far it has traveled in 20 hours, 10 minutes and 28 seconds, since Noon Mark of May 5th.

Calculation by **any** of the methods and tables mentioned will prove that the Sun has moved 0°48'48" since Noon Mark of May 5th, 1856.

Add 0°48'48" to 15°08'12" Taurus (TZ), and the answer is 15°57'00" Taurus (TZ), which is the radix place of Freud's Sun, in the standard zodiac.

Then the conversion to the SZ is made, using the VP, as follows:

Sun's tropical longitude at birth .... 15°57'00" Taurus (TZ)
Add longitude of the VP 7 09 33

                                                                                23 06 33
                                                                                —30 88 33

SIDEREAL LONGITUDE OF RADIX SUN .... 23°06'33" Aries (SZ)

In actual practice, many of the foregoing, painstaking steps are foreshortened into a few salient rows of figures which give the answer with ease.

In like manner, the tropical longitudes of the house cusps and other planets' positions are changed into their sidereal equivalents by the simple expedient of applying the VP of 7°10'. In the present example, we are making direct use of the Campanian house cusps, converting them from their tropical to their sidereal values.

As mentioned earlier, there is at present no conclusive, published table of the Campanian house cusps. These have to be computed, in most cases, either with trigonometry, or by means of the useful instructions and tables given by Alan Leo in his "Casting The Horoscope," a text familiar to most students. However, to spare the student unnecessary time-consuming difficulties, this volume contains a special section entitled, "How To Determine The Campanian House Cusps, Using A Placidian Tables Of Houses." The full instructions and simple tables presented there enable the student to determine quickly the Campanian cusps of the intermediate houses, merely by adding given numbers of degrees to the longitude of the Midheaven as given in the standard Placidian tables of houses in his possession. Using the Campanian system for SZ techniques is not absolutely essential, it must be noted, but those who have studied the question agree unanimously that it is desirable in all instances.

Houses	Tropical Longitude		Sidereal Longitude
	° ′		° ′
Midheaven:	5 ♈ 32	is equivalent to	12 ♓ 42
11th Cusp:	26 ♈ 53	is equivalent to	4 ♈ 03
12th Cusp:	10 ♊ 51	is equivalent to	18 ♉ 01
Ascendant:	28 ♋ 54	is equivalent to	6 ♋ 04
2nd Cusp:	22 ♌ 14	is equivalent to	29 ♋ 24
3rd Cusp:	11 ♍ 13	is equivalent to	18 ♌ 23

Planets		Tropical Longitude		Sidereal Longitude
		° ′		° ′ ″
☉	in	15 ♉ 57	is equivalent to	23 ♈ 06 33
☽	in	9 ♊ 12	is equivalent to	16 ♉ 22
☿	in	27 ♉ 00	is equivalent to	4 ♉ 10
♀	in	25 ♈ 52	is equivalent to	3 ♈ 02
♂	in	3 ♎ 25	is equivalent to	10 ♍ 35
♃	in	29 ♓ 30	is equivalent to	6 ♓ 40
♄	in	27 ♊ 30	is equivalent to	4 ♊ 40
♅	in	20 ♉ 36	is equivalent to	27 ♈ 46
♆	in	19 ♓ 50	is equivalent to	27 ♒ 00
♇	in	4 ♉ 19	is equivalent to	11 ♈ 29

Figures 1 and 2 are the tropical and sidereal versions of Freud's radix. Notice that only the zodiacal designations are changed, the entire pattern of relations within both wheels being identical. Since we now know the SZ positions of the Sun and Moon, it follows that we may proceed with the calculation of the solar and lunar returns, to show the novice-reader how this is done. The process should be already familiar to anybody whose astrological knowledge is sufficient that he does not fall in the "beginner" category. For the solar return, it is best to repair to the use of the helpful "Tables of Diurnal Planetary Motion"; if these are not immediately available, any of the other logarithmic or arithmetical methods may be employed. Lunar returns, on the other hand, are best calculated with the usual D. P. logs with which every student, even the "beginner" is automatically familiar.

Completely dispossessed of home, property, books and papers, when the Nazis invaded Austria, where he resided in Vienna, Freud was ransomed by a princess of Greece and migrated to London where he died on September 23rd, 1939, aged 83. One of the most brilliant scientific minds among the sons of men in this or any other age, Freud had left an impress upon the world as indelible as Darwin's or Galileo's or Aristotle's. His progressed chart for **terminus vitae** was lucid in its indications of death, what with both progressed Moon and progressed Midheaven conjoining his radix Saturn—a typical index of demise. Let us cast the solar and lunar return charts preceding his death, to illustrate the procedure.

Auxiliary Table Showing
Amounts of General Precession for Intervals of Years

Years	Prec.	Years	Prec.	Years	Prec.	Years	Prec.
	° ′		° ′		° ′		° ′
1	0 01	26	0 22	51	0 43	76	1 03
2	0 02	27	0 23	52	0 43	77	1 04
3	0 03	28	0 23	53	0 44	78	1 05
4	0 03	29	0 24	54	0 45	79	1 06
5	0 04	30	0 25	55	0 46	80	1 07
6	0 05	31	0 26	56	0 47	81	1 08
7	0 06	32	0 27	57	0 48	82	1 08
8	0 07	33	0 28	58	0 48	83	1 09
9	0 08	34	0 28	59	0 49	84	1 10
10	0 08	35	0 29	60	0 50	85	1 11
11	0 09	36	0 30	61	0 51	86	1 12
12	0 10	37	0 31	62	0 52	87	1 13
13	0 11	38	0 32	63	0 53	88	1 13
14	0 12	39	0 33	64	0 53	89	1 14
15	0 13	40	0 33	65	0 54	90	1 15
16	0 13	41	0 34	66	0 55	91	1 16
17	0 14	42	0 35	67	0 56	92	1 17
18	0 15	43	0 36	68	0 57	93	1 18
19	0 16	44	0 37	69	0 58	94	1 18
20	0 17	45	0 38	70	0 58	95	1 19
21	0 18	46	0 38	71	0 59	96	1 20
22	0 18	47	0 39	72	1 00	97	1 21
23	0 19	48	0 40	73	1 01	98	1 22
24	0 20	49	0 41	74	1 02	99	1 23
25	0 21	50	0 42	75	1 03	100	1 24

Since the VP regresses about 1° in 72 years, or 50″ per year, it will have traversed about 1°09′ in 83 years, the age of the native when the event in question transpired. An auxiliary table showing the approximate number of minutes of arc of precession for any given number of years is a handy thing to have at one's fingertips, as it serves to short-cut the process of finding the correct date of solunar returns. We present such a brief table herewith. However, an easily-remembered rule will do the trick equally well. From the age in years, subtract 1/6 of the age; the resulting number gives the approximate amount of precession having ensued in the life to date. Hence, 83 minus one-sixth of 83, or 14, is 69, or 1°09′. By "approximate," we mean that the possible error involved in this little trick never exceeds one minute of arc over several centuries.

Since the native died, aged 83, and we know that 1°09′ has precessed since birth, we add this amount to the **tropical** longitude of the radix Sun to learn what its approximate tropical longitude is on the date of its return to the point in **sidereal** longitude it held at birth.

Freud's radix Sun	=	15°57′ Taurus (TZ)
Add precession	=	1 09
Approx. TZ at Return	=	17 06 Taurus (TZ).

Consulting a Greenwich Noon ephemeris for year of demise, 1939, we find that the Sun transits 17°06′ Taurus between the noons of May 8th and 9th.

The Sun's daily motion, 0°58′01″, on May 8th, is extracted.

The Sun's TZ longitude at noon on May 8th is converted to SZ longitude by applying the VP which is found to be 5°59′51″ Pisces.

The Sun's SZ longitude at noon on May 8th is then subtracted from the radix SZ longitude of the Sun, the difference being the distance it must travel from noon to "return" to its natal position.

Sun's TZ noon position, May 8th	17°00′04″	Taurus	(TZ)
Plus VP	5 59 51		
Gives Sun's SZ noon position, May 8th	22 59 55	Aries	(SZ)
Sun's SZ radix longitude	23°06′33″	Aries	(SZ)
Minus Sun's SZ longitude, noon, 8th	22 59 55	Aries	(SZ)
Yields distance required	0 06 38		

Having the two values, daily motion and distance, you can quickly determine the Greenwich Mean Time of the solar return, by using any of the systems mentioned earlier (each of which requires tables, which carry their own instructions).

In any case, the answer will be that the solar return occurs at 2h44m38s past Greenwich Noon on May 8th, 1939. (For all practical purposes, the nearest minute is sufficient, as the express **number of odd seconds is a spurious step.** Hence, the time of Freud's last solar return is 2:45 P. M., G. M. T., May 8th, 1939.) Since the native was in London, no longitude reduction, to get Local Mean Time, is necessary. The sidereal time of his solar return chart is then determined to be 5:46:45, by the usual method. The planet's positions are derived from the ephemeris using the constant log 0.94182, or, if the convenient "Tables of Diurnal Planetary Motion" are employed, by direct use of the G. M. T.

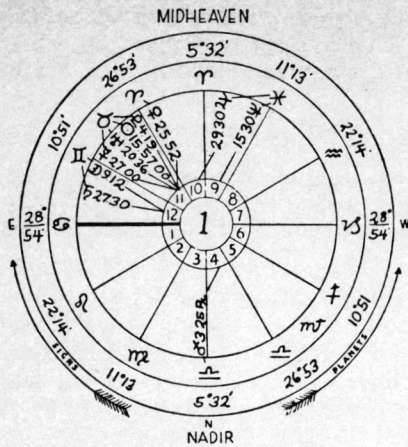

Radix of Sigmund Freud
Tropical Zodiac Version
May 6, 1856
9:23 A. M., L.M.T.
Freiberg, Czechoslovakia

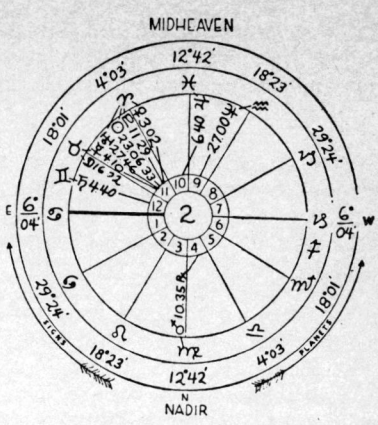

Radix of Sigmund Freud
Sidereal Zodiac Version
May 6, 1856
9:23 A. M., L.M.T.
Freiberg, Czechoslovakia

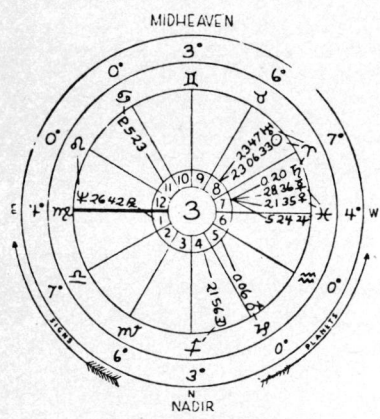

Freud's Solar Return
Preceding Demise
May 8, 1939
2:45 P. M., L.M.T.
London, England

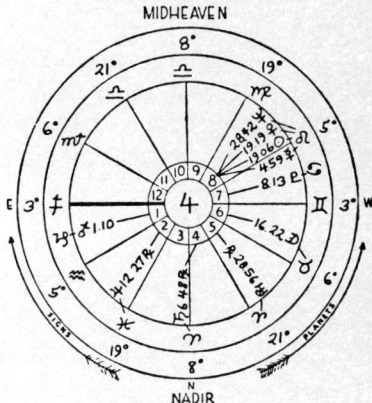

Freud's Lunar Return
Preceding Demise
September 6, 1939
3:01 P. M., L.M.T.
London, England

Notice in the solar return chart the remarkable indices of death. The Sun and Uranus are conjunct in the 8th house, applying by 0°40′, while the planets Mars and Saturn are within 0°14′ partile square, the latter malefic being angular. Also in the foreground is the Moon in

— 25 —

the 4th house—"end of life"—configurated with rising Neptune. Under the circumstances, if you had been handed this chart, knowing that the native was advanced in years, what would you have said it signified?

Lunar returns, while more powerful in immediate effect, are subservient to the preceding solar return. Therefore, we must look to the lunar return just preceding Freud's passing for proof that lunar returns usually "time" the major occurrences foreshadowed in the annual chart.

The radix tropical longitude of Freud's Moon was 9°12′ Gemini. To this we add the approximate amount of precession since birth, 1°09′, and find that the lunar return for death must occur on the day when last the Moon was in 10°21′ Gemini (TZ). Scanning the ephemeris page for dates prior to September 23rd, 1939, when the death took place, we note that the Moon transitted its radix position between the Greenwich noons of September 6th and 7th. The VP for September 6th is 6°00′ Pisces. The same steps are taken, but with far less effort, as those for the solar return. Calculation of the lunar return is accomplished so readily, using Diurnal Proportional Logarithms, that the process will not be difficult, even for the merest beginner.

Moon's TZ noon longitude, Sept. 6th	8°41′ Gemini	(TZ)
Add VP	6 00	
Moon's SZ noon longitude, Sept. 6th	14 41 Taurus	(SZ)
Radix SZ longitude of Moon	16 22 Taurus	(SZ)
Minus Moon's SZ noon longitude, 6th	14 41 Taurus	(SZ)
Yields distance required	1 41	

The next step, to find the G. M. T. of the lunar return, is an old familiar procedure to every astrological student.

D.P. log 1°41′ =	1.15404	(= log of distance)
Minus D.P. log 13°23′ =	0.25365	(= log of daily motion)
D.P. log G.M.T. =	0.90039	

Now, 0.90039 is the diurnal proportional logarithm of 3h01m after noon. So the time of lunar return is 3:01 P. M., G. M. T., September 6th, 1939.

The planets' positions are therefore found as of 3:01 P. M., using the constant log 0.90039. The sidereal time of the lunar return is reckoned to be 14h00m, with which we enter the London table of houses. Figure 4 is the resulting return chart, converted to terms of the sidereal zodiac. Again the Sun resides in the 8th house, while the Moon in the 6th suggests depletion of the vital energies. Most striking of all is the great T-square of angular ("foreground") malefic planets: Saturn conjunct the Nadir, Mars rising, and Pluto in the 7th.

The three benefic planets, Venus, Jupiter and Uranus, are in middle-ground positions and therefore cannot perceptibly offset the inimical influences of foreground malefics. We realize, however, that the novice is not yet prepared for the more delightful task of solunar interpretation, so must introduce him to it here and now.

Note on Accuracy: The student will be glad to hear that the extent of accuracy required in casting birthcharts and progressing them is not called for in solunar work. The sidereal time of solunar return charts cannot possibly be determined to the correct second, as the local mean time of the return can really never be got to seconds, and there is also a margin of error, for lunar returns in particular, of two or three minutes, due to the fact that lunar motion is not uniform. We suggest the using of tenths of minutes for finding the sidereal time, but the result must be "rounded off" to the nearest whole minute when the table of houses is entered for cusps. Then the cusps, written as whole degrees, are as nearly correct as practicability warrants. In general work, it is not even expedient to enter planetary positions to the minute into a wheel, for these may also be rounded off.

Anent this matter of "whole degrees," we want to emphasize the mathematically correct way to designate positions. If a body is anywhere between 0°01′ and 1°00′, it is in the first degree, and, in inserting it in a blank chart, it should be read as 1°, and not "zero degrees." Likewise, when a planet is, say, at 29°16′ of a sign or constellation, it is actually in the thirtieth degree, and, in inserting its position in a chart, it must be written 30°. This is a matter which many textbooks have failed to teach the student. When you are "rounding off to the nearest degree," you are actually identifying the category or class-interval in which it is located. Therefore, the correct name of the degree in which it is placed should be used, and not that of the preceding degree. Those who might take issue with us on this point evidently "push forward" into the next sign a planet anywhere between 29°31′ and 29°59′ of a sign, if they are "rounding off."

CHAPTER 3

SOLUNAR INTERPRETATION: THE SUN

THE SUN signifies "the Self," and as such indicates the ego and the will of the native. It is the "I," distinct from the lunar "Not-I." In simpler terms, the significance of the Sun in solunar charts is that of **the native himself,** while its position and aspects refer to the native's **self-assertions.** Self-assertion is necessarily the expression of **desire,** for which reason we say the Sun represents "the heart," in the esthetical sense of the word. An "act of self" is any movement produced voluntarily by the native, without the command or coercion of others. If one tells a deliberate lie, it is an act-of-self, as a falsehood emanates from him. But if one is lied to, a falsehood is directed toward him. Solar indications, then, are suggestive of things the native himself **will perpetrate** during the period covered by the prognosis of a return chart. Lunar indications, conversely, denote events which **happen to** him.

The Sun corroborates—even activates—progressed aspects more strongly than any other body, since all progressions denote self-assertions in much the same manner. On the surface, it may appear that solar indications are capable of producing events apart from the native's precipitation of them. Closer analysis, however, always proves that the individual actually brought them about. For instance, a Sun-Mars conjunction on the descendant in a solunar return preceding a man's arrest, or his murder, might suggest that our consignment of solar indications to the realm of acts-of-self is illogical in the light of subsequent events. Yet, being arrested is an eventuality brought about by his own impetuous transgression of law. Or, his murder is the result of his own intolerable unruliness or cruelty or retaliation.

The Sun's house position tells us where the native stands, from what situation he views the outside world, and to what milieu or environmental circumstances he surrenders his individuality during the interval concerned. Its primary meaning is that of **desire,** remember. Following the sidereal technique which classifies the twelve houses into three groups of four constituents each, in order of their relative importance, let us turn our attentions first to the Sun's mundane position.

The Sun in the Foreground. The Sun in the **1st house** is in its most vitalizing position. Here, there is no "surrender of individuality," no fusing of interest with others on a reciprocal basis. By itself, it means self-aggrandizement and heroism. The native precipitates circumstances which will call the attention of outsiders to his personality and desirability. It denotes a period when self-interest is so intensified, the native may seem oblivious to the welfare or feelings of others. **His** feelings, **his** belongings, **his** welfare come first in all considerations, excepting where sexuality and its outlets are involved, when the exigency may occasion a seemingly genuine interest in others. Pride and vitality, both keywords of a rising Sun, keynote the month or year in question (pride more particularly with solar charts, vitality more particularly with lunars). The native in any case will show a decided orientation to the passing moment, rather than to the past or future. The 1st house stands for the Here and Now. With childlike simplicity, he will respond to every eventuality around him in typically extroverted manner.

The Sun in the **4th house** is a withdrawal of scattered forces and outside compunctions, so that the native banks solely upon his own assets and abilities for any sort of accomplishment. Inasmuch as this position enlivens the "pater familias" complex, the native may manifest and feel a definite self-importance out of all proportion to his mediocrity as a mere earth-inhabitant. Hence, he becomes "a lone wolf" so far as enterprises are concerned, taking no one into his confidence. Whatever "surrender of individuality" there might be is to the exigencies of home life, one's own backyard, as it were. It usually denotes that the native, through choice and action of his own, will bring about the finis of some major cycle in his life, such as moving to a different city, or resigning every former fraternal tie, in lieu of new interests and opportunities. His orientation, mentally, is toward the future (whereas the immediate present, or "youth," fixes his outlook in the 1st house), toward what will be if he does so and so, or if that or this happens, etc. A useful keyword for a 4th-house Sun is "self-rehabilitation." Naturally, he will concern himself with 4th-house factors and filial problems while the direct focus of his selfhood, the Sun, is embedded in the appropriate sector of the horoscope.

The Sun in the **7th house** denotes a natural gravitation toward others. The native surrenders his individuality to the exigencies of worldly life. Because the Sun represents "the heart," the native's emotional energy is re-charged, together with his self-confidence. It follows that the self-assertion which characterizes angularity of the Sun's position will be mainly directed toward the native's preferred love-object, usually the opposite sex. Matters related to the descendant occupy his attention; keywords of this house are co-operation and competition. The native throws his entire weight into worldly ambitions, with strong personal fervor in behalf of a rightful share in the spoils. Angularity of the Sun always increases the vital reserve, and for health matters is a definite asset. The native is capable of feeling and behaving as others do, as the self-consciousness shifts to a fuller appreciation of humane values. Sexually and matrimonially, the native's own narcissism is a guiding factor, and he selects his erotic contacts by their appeal to his own vanity rather than their singular desirability.

The Sun in the **10th** incites all-around self-expression as no other position of the luminary can do, but within special confines. The native is forced or cajoled to surrender his individuality to the exigencies imposed upon him by powers greater or higher than his own. (A typical position of a person at the mercy of a court or prospective employer.) His attitude toward others is that of sincere patronage and support of socially approved institutions and traditions. He seeks to glorify himself by mingling with higher social levels than his background would normally allow; he speaks familiarly of famous people, as his whole demeanor focuses in this compulsion to appear more unique than he really is. (Actual ambition and honor is a purely Jupiterian matter, not to be confused with the self-glorification or **wide attention** paid him by the Sun's elevation.) A man or woman whose current Sun is in the 10th house would be a wise appointee for organizational or promotional work, as the managerial ability is enhanced, and persistent interest in the responsibilities entailed will not wane during the chart-period considered.

The Sun in the Middleground. Middleground solar positions are those "only average" in their consummate significance. Yet, all positions are unique, within themselves and their context, in horoscopy. With the Sun in any succedent house, the native's egocentricity is lodged midway between the crowd and total seclusion, so to speak. That is, he evinces no overwhelming drive for being seen and heard, but rather has a compulsion to be felt and handled. (Cadent-house positions denote a desire to be served and left alone.) No great upsurge of vitality animates him to heroism or to a heel-striking, arm-swinging gait, catching to the eyes of passers-by. His sentimental nature is prone to be confined to the more naive end-aims of life, such as comfort, sex and diversion, taken in average-sized dozes.

The Sun in the **2nd house** places a practical emphasis on the importance of security, the value of coin, and the desirability of shrewdness in capitalizing on circumstances as they arise. The native surrenders his individuality to the exigencies of comfort and security. He often tends toward the "arty" way of living, letting his senses be the sole determinator of decision and action. The primary inference of this position is that of its keynote: individual resources. "The king is in his counting house, counting out his money...." The native's overt traits are possessiveness and reticence where the reward for effort is not objective.

A **5th-house** Sun, on the other hand, indicates arousal to participate in activities the rewards from which are subjective, ever so subtile. The native does this thing, or that, for the sheer "fun of it." Again, we have a surrender of individuality to the direction of the senses, an unerring alignment of the self with the line running from pain to pleasure. He is unencumbered by worry or discontent so long as affairs run along smoothly. Of course, because this house pertains to the pursuit of pleasure, the Sun here is a token of prodigality, even of dissipation, in the common meaning of those terms. The native is apt to waste his attention and favors on unworthy persons or things, in the eyes of others, but any such disapproval is merely the upholding of social mores. When Oscar Wilde said, "Pleasure is the only thing worth living for," he was voicing a truth which has stung the egos of cerebrotonics since civilization began. Basically, the 5th is the house of eroticism, which in turn is mainly autoeroticism, if strict definitions are adhered to. Pride in the sensuous charms of the physical self is kindled with the Sun in the 5th. A decided yen to improve the attractiveness of the appearance is coincident with a 5th-house Sun. Furthermore, matters traditionally associated with this segment of the chart are highlighted in the native's consciousness during the period in question. Hence, he asserts himself as an entertainer, and any artistic talent he may have is brought out further into the open, showing decided improvement and greater promise. (Here again is an example of the kinship of progressions and solar-return factors.) Eager to learn new things, he is unashamed to admit his erstwhile ignorance in a quest for information or suggestions.

An **8th-house** Sun signifies the resignation of the self to a kind of "destiny-idea" (in Oswald Spengler's sense of the term), in which the individual finds a rational, encouraging explanation for everything, especially the misfortunes, which happen to him. This position is one of the most difficult to delineate, failing to define, as it does, a distinct department of life in the scheme of things. It has a definite bearing upon obscenity, to be sure, but obscenity in most instances is an honest acceptance of the real state of affairs. We have noticed that an 8th-house Sun in return charts coincides with a self-incurred humility, through an awkward confession of love, or conflicts over secret "vices" (distinguished from the neurotic self-belittlement of Neptune). The native gives much thought to the eternal riddles of death and deity; religious conversion is not unlikely under such an influence. Traditional 8th-house secretiveness effronts itself in moving the native to live a "double life," in order to escape judgment by those steeped hopelessly in conventional attitudes. Therefore, it is not unusual to find a native, highly esteemed by his associates for conscientious religious participation, secretly stealing away to enjoy the less artificial pleasures of a tryst. Other 8th-house connectives, ranging from life-insurance subscription to legacies and loans, may engage the native's interest.

In the popular vernaculer, the **11th house** rules "friends, hopes and wishes." More truly, this means one's relation to group attitudes, his imagination, and his vicarious experiences. The Sun here points to a suppression of individual motives in behalf of self-survival by means of protecting the welfare of the group. More bluntly, the native surrenders his personal attitude to the opinion of the people in his immediate circle, with a juvenile sort of faithfulness. He sees the advantage of not departing from the accepted pattern or expected behavior. He is strangely skewed to the adoption of new resolutions, the taking of oaths, etc. The 11th house is anybody's "audience," for it is from this sector of the chart that enthusiasm is warmed. So far as all-around fortune is concerned, the 11th house is a preferred position for the Sun. Planets in the 11th usually hint what kind of longings are fulfilled during the return-period charted. The basic function of the 11th house is "to organize"; for every period lived by the native with the Sun here, the end of each period always chalks up to his credit a further improvement, organization, or integration of his social status.

The Sun in the Background. Cadent positions of the Sun are unimportant in many ways, the main exception being the adverse effects they have on the health. The least favorable health-house is the 6th, for the Sun there denotes a greatly diminished amount of "animal heat." The Sun in any cadent house indicates a retirement of the self away from big objectives in life, so that the native contents himself with passive entanglement in the skein of endless trivialities. It is difficult to be at all productive or energetic. The things traditionally ascribed to the rulerships of the 3rd, 6th, 9th and 12th houses, will engage the native's interest or become his tramping-grounds, but, for the most part, little weight should be attached to background positions. This rule applies to all other planets as well: the background smothers their effectiveness.

Solar Aspects

With the **Moon** in aspect to the Sun, particularly square or opposition, egoism is even more intensified, although little "individuality" as such may be shown, as the native is eager for the approval and attention of others. His relationship to the general milieu is vivified, so that he may confidently seek or chance to meet persons of social and business importance. A Sun-Moon conjunction brings the native face-to-face with person-to-person realities. There is little rest or seclusion for him when this happens; he is swept along in a floodtide of activities, engagements and conventions. Everything he does has a recoil of equal force; if he strikes someone, he is hit back with fierce retaliation (cf. Mars), as the conjunction of the Lights is a token of reciprocity. Sun-conjunct-Moon is a very adverse indication, to most ways of thinking, for it is a too great bundling of energies, not allowing "moderation" of any kind, so that things have a trying tendency to get out of hand. Sun-Moon configurations denote people and things **coming to** the native. Hence, **he receives** invitations, messages, citations, awards, congratulations, even curses, and the like. With the Lights rising, such commendation from others will most likely be from heroic deeds or singular achievements. An opposition of the luminaries always denotes that an acme has been reached in the native's present cycle, so that the chart-period will be one of culmination rather than commencement.

A conjunction of the Sun and **Mercury** (within 3° to be considered powerful) naturally reinforces all solar indications—gives them wings, as it were. It shows reliance upon one's repertoire, rather than originality, inasmuch as Mercury always implies **habit** and objective thinking. Mercury at elongation, farthest from the Sun, shows ability to think unbiasedly, above and beyond social mores and mental stereotypes, we believe. Hence, in solar conjunction, the reverse may be true, and the native thinks and acts automatically, in accordance with the preconceptions and notions he deems factual. In the introvert, Mercury-Sun conjunctions herald periods of extraordinary outflow of self so that he becomes what is poetically described as "an open book" to others. He is moved to pen his thoughts, in correspondence, diary or articles, and does not suppress the desire to say exactly what he thinks.

Sun-Venus conjunctions are narcissistic, in that they refract the libido toward the self. Self-satisfaction, then, is the initial meaning of a conjunction of the egocentric Sun and the loving Venus. The orb of this conjunction, to be markedly effective, should be confined to about 5°, although the astrologer is left to decide such marginal allowances for himself as he sees fit. When Venus is distant from the Sun, say, in excess of 40°, the elongation by its very nature symbolizes a liberation of the emotions from pure self-centeredness. Hence, compassion for others may be the reaction. It more commonly may be taken to show that the native's thinking and acting are peculiarly free from commitments to others and from the blinding glare of seriously personal attachments. His amorous interests are shoved into the hinterland at this time, in quest of more worldly ambitions.

With the Sun angular, any of the five major aspects to **Mars** is important, for they have a direct bearing upon the physical organism. Sol-Mars conjunctions denote, first of all, a burning zeal for self-satisfaction through aggression, sex, fighting, and the destruction of obstacles and opponents. Irrational to the extreme, the Spartan-type of native has a "to the kill!" compulsion, is fearless, delights in behaving as a roughneck, and often occupies himself with firearms, knives, and the like, for the imaginative excitement such diversion offers. Persons under such influence appear bent on assault, step deliberately on ants, lose their tempers easily, and provoke fighting moods in others. Their attitude is that might makes right, and a native so affected is apt to forget or belittle the more wholesome morals learned at mother's knee or Sunday School.

Squares between the Sun and Mars particularize the object toward which the native's passing ire is aimed, and the battlefield on which his furiousness is spent. Mars in the 11th, for instance, in aspect to the Sun, suggests self-incurred disputes with friends and counsellors, who often prove co-operative in accepting the challenge, to the native's own detriment. With Mars in the 10th, his superiors are the target, and, often, the boomerang. The natural heroistic leanings of Sol, coupled with the criminogenic nature of Mars and the quadrature aspect, gives him a kind of Robin Hood complex, if not a Napoleonic one. With Mars in the 9th, square Sun, a definite intolerance toward the beatitudnal way of life is in evidence. Mars in the 3rd and solar aspect places the object of assault in the immediate milieu, i.e., blood relatives, neighbors, the bus driver, the delivery boy, and what-have-you in the way of 3rd-house connectives. Things and persons ordinarily taken for granted arouse the native's temper and challenges. When the square is wholly angular, with Mars in the 4th, warn his family that there is a bull in their china closet. Psychoanalysis teaches that filial relations are ambivalent, that for every strong love in the conscious mind, there is an equally strong unconscious hate, and vice versa. This being true, outcroppings of the repressed, negative sides of one's feelings toward his immediate family members may be expected. Lifelong docile obedience to a strict parent may end abruptly with a temperamental, even physical explosion by the native theretofore insufficiently equipped with Sun-Mars power to make a break. In certain cases, unusually strong incestuous tendencies may be heated so that they rise to the surface of consciousness, for Mars denotes the libidinous passions as well. Mars in the 5th in solar configuration has the connotation, clearly, of hotly aroused eroticism, minus the truly blissful foreplay or tender musings which are the token of Venus. Personality-type permitting, the pursuits of the native along this line may give rise to urges akin to priapism. He becomes a Don Juan, she, a Messalina, if circumstances permit of direct outlet (cf. 7th house).

An opposition of the Sun and Mars across the horizon of a chart signifies that combative impulses often overwhelm the native, and he may survive the chart-period with many wounds to lick. In any case, there is a zest for competition, for the pitting of strength against strength. Innately reckless under this influence, the native delights in risk to impress others as well as to hallow his self-importance. The attempting of hair-raising feats is probable (successful if lunar or other indications portend avoidance of injury or defeat, disastrous if to the contrary). Mars in the 8th in solar aspect implies a disregard for the rights of others and their property and assets, and a tendency toward more than ordinary obscenity and anal-sadism.

The sextiles and trines of the Sun and Mars serve to reinforce the vitality, whet the sensual appetites, and cause the native to live spiritedly, indulging his primitive desires at will. Less crude or bombastic in action than the square or opposition, nevertheless, the 60° and 120° formations of these fiery bodies are by no means benefic, in sidereal astrology. (Two murderers, to our immediate knowledge, performed their ghastly deeds under Sun-Mars trines.) Generally, Mars in any configuration with the Sun is inhibition-releasing in effect. Inhibitions are simply dams which block and hence suppress primitive aggression and rapacity, imposed by civilization during growth from infancy to adulthood. With Mars thus made active, breaches in the suppressing wall are dug, allowing untempered animalism to flow into consciousness. In the more highly developed sort of person, Sun-Mars aspects conduce toward construction, mechanical ingenuity, and the spending of much energy in rigorous work. He will seek to clear the jungle, unlike the less-cultured types who will roam it. The locale or objective through which the native releases the activated Martian energies is shown by the position of the planet. Distinguish squares and oppositions from sextiles and trines by assuming the latter to be less blind, more premeditated, less climacteric, and more intentional. Thus, Mars in the 5th, trine rising Sun, may be excessively excitable to the passions, but does not conduce toward such strong satyriasis as that by the square aspect; firmness rather than brutality is used to succor the desires.

Solar aspects of **Jupiter,** with the Sun in the foreground, are the most ambition-goading configurations of all, so far as worldly standards are concerned. In sidereal astrology, Jupiter retains its reputation as the "Greater Benefic," which has made it the favorite component in tropical astrology. A conjunction of Sol and Jupiter signifies boundless enthusiasm in the native, together with a munificence of viewpoint which leads him toward self-improvement, socially and financially. He is apt to adopt an extreme rightist political viewpoint, since this configuration is essentially royalistc, imperialistic, and regal. Indiscriminately amiable, generous and tolerant in a pompous sort of way, his foremost craving is for comfort and coin. His sexual appetite is low and relatively weak, as centralized eroticism gives way to over-all complacency and compassion regarding the world and people about him. In action, he is opportunistic, and appears to do things and engage himself in such a way as to profit both in money and friendships.

Squares to Jupiter by the Sun are splendid dynamics for enhancing one's self and station in life. Should Jupiter be angular, one's efforts toward betterment are "out in the world" and society. If in the 4th house, the aspect works itself out less far afield than if it were in the 7th and 10th. Always read the meaning of Sun-Jupiter formations by assuming that the native "is interested in" the welfare of that person or category shown by Jupiter's position. This focus of the philanthropic interest reciprocates in kind, netting the native praise and profit from that quarter of existence indicated. The opposition is best where purely business ventures are concerned. Jupiter angular in a solunar return chart is always to be taken as an augury of gain and increase, in ways revealed by its aspects and relationships. Do not forget that solar aspects primarily denote acts-of-self. Thus, Jupiter related with Sol always charges the native with desires for enhancing his own lot by the acquisition of money or honors, usually both. In persons whose super-ego is weak, this planetary combination may even result in the acquiring of money by devious methods, even robbery or chicanery. Squares and oppositions give tremendous impetus to the desire for more money; sextiles and trines, always less energizing and more deliberate in action, give the native the power of forethought and smoother emotional flux, so that he makes fewer mistakes and is more clever in his drive for "bigger and better" things. Too, he is more convincingly sincere in the eyes of others, so that his obvious compulsive acquisitiveness is taken by others to be only a keen and admirable economic-intelligence.

Not so with **Sun-Saturn** relationships, which in many ways are polar in action to Sun-Jupiter. A conjunction of Sun and Saturn in the foreground is the earmark of the miser or witch-burner. Self-restraint is the keynote of this conjunction, for the native imposes upon himself more than logical disciplines and limitations. There is a primary need for privacy and freedom from interference by others. In cases which we have encountered, Saturn seems always to relate to religious conviction, so that the native may revive even a completely recanted orthodox faith while under its influence. He becomes more prudish and squeamish where morals are concerned, thereby causing others close to him unfair discomfort under his scrutiny. He criticizes his friends and associates for surprisingly petty reasons, and his sensitivity to the feelings of others seems dulled.

Squares between Sol and Saturn denote that the native goes to extremes in his restraint of feelings, irking those persons represented by the house which Saturn occupies. They also show to what subjects he does his whining, as well as for what purpose. If Saturn is in the 11th, his friends and club-fellows suffer the imposition; if Saturn is in the 10th, his selfishness and criticism is aimed at superiors; if Saturn is in the 9th, his over-intensity and disgust is directed toward nominal religions and education, in which case fault-finding and vetoing find a target safer to attack, as little is risked. If Saturn is in the 3rd, he cancels subscriptions and services as being overhead expenses, for his thriftiness at this time is almost fanatic. In the 4th, the period covered by the chart in question finds his family peculiarly refused even customary favors. With Saturn in the 5th, his pursuits of pleasure are brought to a standstill, or else restricted to objective genitality without consideration for the partner concerned.

Saturn in configuration with the Sun is always an indication that the native says "No!" to whatever parties its house-location describes. A veritable crank for the time being, the native is uncooperative, reclusive, shorn of personal attractiveness (through self-neglect, usually), and bitter toward life in general. Friends and relatives wonder, "What's wrong with him, anyway?" Sun-opposition-Saturn across the horizon houses is lethal to the native's ambitions or marital interests. Discourteous and cantankerous, he will not be in an agreeable mood, so to approach him for patronage or solicit his support for any organized cause is often futile, turned down with the glib quip that "missionary work begins at home," or, "what's there in it for me?" etc. Needless to mention, too, Sun-Saturn formations are extremely unfortunate to the health, with particular effects on the heart and blood pressure. In lunar returns, we have found Sun-square-Saturn to denote sidereal months of anxiety (in the psychoanalytic sense of the word, derived as it is from "der Angst," which is German for "fear"). As is to be expected, the native provokes the anxiety-producing situation himself (which amounts to nerve-wracking proportions if Pluto is in the foreground). A good keyword for Sun-Saturn effects is "punishment" for acts-of-self or Saturnian attitudes.

One of the best tonics for a case of prolonged blues and disgruntlement over the dullness of life is to find one's self the happy recipient of a foreground **Uranus** configurated with another benefic. Aspects of the Sun and Uranus spur the native to liveliness, spontaniety and eagerness for change. Not content to stay in a stereotyped surrounding or with commonplace interests, he yields to a heart-felt desire for freedom from restraint, obligation and convention. Suddenly, he discovers to his own amazement, his habitual tastes and manner of living lack color and appeal. As a reaction to this realization, his restless, seeking mind covetously scans that greener grass on the other side of the fence. He feels the urge to break away from routine, to travel away from familiar, boring scenes, and re-route his social interests into more fascinating by-paths. Remembering the thrills and adventures of his youth, he yearns to recapture the gaiety and sparkle of those Green Years.

A conjunction of Sol and Uranus, first of all, denotes self-discovery. Next, it tells that the native will strive to revamp his whole routine of living so that he may be able to make more progress. For example, he may realize that the flux of social visitors to his home detrimentally interferes with his own plans, work and pastimes; a brisk "housecleaning" among his acquaintances usually follows. Breaking off of old ties is a famous token of Sun-Uranus. Another noteworthy effect of this influence calls forth that rugged or refined individuality, whatever the case may be, which causes others to remark of the native, "I didn't know he had it in him," or, "That's a side to his nature we didn't know existed—will wonders never cease!" The astrologer may exclaim "Novus Ordo!" whenever he encounters a chart having such a conjunction.

Always read Uranus as "the thrill planet," for its very essence is pleasurable excitement (unlike Martian excitement which stems from fear of possible disaster, e.g., break-neck speeding, stunt flying, aerial acrobatics, etc.). The kind of thrill that Uranus augments is of the nature of adventure, discovery, doing things that are forbidden by society, and the throes of orgasm. Therefore, when the Sun throws a square or opposition to Uranus, especially in the foreground of a solunar chart, the native throws his whole being into the pursuit of Thrill. Even while such aspects pose problems, particularly of adjustment, they are beneficial to the native's emotional wellbeing Sun-Uranus vibrations are splendid remedies for emotional stagnation and mental fixity, as they save the native from that proverbial rut of one-track thinking and cloistered feelings. In every Sun-Uranus association, the house position concerned points to the locale where "changes" are made. Where worldly affairs are entailed, Sun-Uranus is excellent for organizing, making basic innovations in method, and putting new ideas to work. It is not attuned, however, to partnerships or unions.

Trines and sextiles of the Sun to Uranus are less abrupt in action than the other major configurations. They instill in the native that same zest for living and thrilling experiences, but lend to the over-all picture that trait now popularly called "the hormone look" (!). There is more wholesomeness, more sincere sparkle in the native's personality at this time, so that he does not step on the toes of other people to satiate his impulses. He tempers the ever-present Uranian sarcasm with witticisms which do not offend. Originality, cleverness, and smooth persuasiveness achieve for him the ends he seeks, for no finer personality-priming influence can be found than that of Sun-Uranus in trine or sextile formation. Oppositions suggest the seeking of remote objects, i.e., those things ordinarily out of reach of the native in his everyday habitat. Conjunctions call attention to the discovery of new delights and knowledge in and around the familiar base of operations.

Aspects of the Sun to **Neptune** are especially interesting. They always augur a desperation of feelings which may give rise to disastrous attempts to lie, misrepresent, glamorize or fictionalize one's self. The native lets his imagination wander awry in the fascinating dream-word of "delusions of grandeur," and is apt to incur the ridicule of those whom he intends to impress with his envious "background" and/or assets. False accents, affections of aristocracy, and nose-wrinkling at the mere sight of bugs or garbage, are typical signs of Sun-Neptune vanity. In a frantic effort to defend private interests, the native may go to a ridiculous extreme by telling falsehoods which he believes will serve to secure his ends. The square aspect, in particular, identifies the scene of action, Neptune's house-position pointing to the victim of his machinations. If Neptune is in the 4th, a parent is lied to; if in the 5th, his or her sweetheart becomes the dupe. A 10th-house Neptune suggests a superior, either parental or official, while the 11th may involve a friend, etc., the 7th "taking" the marital or business partner.

A conjunction of the Sun and Neptune is obviously the surest omen of self-delusion, of the neurotic flight-from-reality kind. The native is bound determined, unconsciously, not to recognize aspects of reality in any relationship, for in doing so, his idols are at stake. He keeps himself a veritable prisoner to his fancies and malpractices, no matter how impractical or injurious they may be, in a sort of masochistic, self-sacrificing way. He becomes his own Svengali, trussed up inescapably in the web of his own undoing. Apart from the conjunction, the other potent aspects (square and opposition) promote this same Svengali-Trilby circumstance, only another person is the unfortunate Trilby, subjected to a humiliation which the native causes. Since Neptune always signifies despair and resignation, the native invariably suffers victimization and loss through his own intrigues. In a recent case brought to our attention, we found Sun-Neptune to coincide with sexual thraldom—a thraldom mistaken by the native for genuine love. Another characteristic Sun-Neptune expression is a "persecution complex," brought about through the sinister forebodings and suspicions which the native appears to feel while under this influence.

Less baneful are the sextiles and trines of Sol and Neptune. To be sure, the desperation and masochistic trends inherent in this planetary match are present, but to a lesser, more passive degree. The native projects to the outside his own hopes and fears, in the form of Christs and Satans, with whom he may often be on familiar speaking terms (if an introvert), but with less emotional energy-charge than he feels under the square or opposition when these projections are onto his employer, government officials or dead relatives. Gripped by a sense of inadequacy, the native under this influence feels a frantic need to be revved up; he may take flight to a psychiatrist, his religious overseer, or a public counsellor, for advice. His confession, of course, will be more colorful and padded than cold, sobre truth, but the act will doubtless do more good than if he stays bottled up. (Joshua Loth Liebman, that giver of "Peace of Mind" to millions, said something to the effect that a boiling teapot, if sealed up, can wreck a house, but if given only a little outlet, it will sing and sing!) Among other effects of Sun-Neptune combinations are the predisposition toward laziness and suctorial imposition on others. Through vulnerability to upset and constant worrisome jealousy or suspicion, the native may "poison" himself toxically. That feeling in the pit of the stomach that makes one's saliva in turn taste like he had eaten a soggy newspaper is most definitely a typical Sun-Neptune reaction.

In many respects, **Pluto** is the opposite of Neptune, particularly in the way it bangs the gavel of reality when in aspect to the Sun. Nearly as dramatic as Sun-Neptune combinations, Sun-Pluto in no way tolerates the wooziness or illusionary drift of thoughts which accompanies the former. Pluto is life's "wages." With the Sun conjunct Pluto, the native has to "put up or shut up," for he cannot talk his way into or out of anything, or laugh off any consequences for his actions. Hence, Sun-Pluto aspects, particularly the conjunction, imply turning-points in the life, the closing of old cycles and the birth of new. Usually, the native is obtrusive in his making sure that the grand finale or first curtain is a dramatic success, for Sun-Pluto is the dramatizer of events.

Squares and oppositions of the Sun and Pluto always point to the presence of a disrespect for the law, the feelings of others, and sometimes the worthiness of causes and charitable movements. The native shows a distaste of ceremony and social taboos, and discounts the importance of anything or anybody not directly agreeing with or pertaining to his own welfare. There is a noticeable callousness to his attitude, as though he resents the presence of the poor and disabled in society. Impatient to the extreme, nervously taut, he appears on the verge of "cracking" under the strain of somehow being unable to strike a happy medium in anything he says or does or thinks. (Indeed, nervous breakdowns seldom occur without the "last straw" coming about through Pluto's influence. Consecutive solunar returns with Pluto prominent clearly show the evolution of serious mental breakdowns and hysterias.)

Sextiles and trines of Sun-Pluto are auguries of show-downs in the life, usually sponsored by the native himself. He makes important, far-reaching decisions, such as marriage proposals, the buying or selling of property or copyrights, citizenship changes, residential moves, or what-have-you in the way of climacteric acts-of-self. There is nothing spurious or hesitant in Sun-Pluto relationships, no two ways about anything, nor is circumlocution permitted in any way. Decisions are made quickly; action following them is swift and conclusive. A native's whole life may suddenly and dramatically change under the ægis of a foreground Sun-Pluto configuration.

CHAPTER 4

SOLUNAR INTERPRETATION: THE MOON

BY FAR the most important body in solunar charts is the Moon, for it shows by its position and aspects those things which happen to or arouse the native quite independently of his own desires in the matter. Hence, it denotes **involuntary action**. It provokes the events and circumstances which are **forced upon** the native, although they are beyond his ken until their impact in his life and moods is felt. The primary meaning of Luna is that of **sensation and response**. For instance, if the Moon is configurated with Venus, the native sensibly responds to the erotic possibilities of a situation which arises (usually the meeting of another interested person). But if the formation is between the Moon and Mars, the imminent response to a situation is sensibly painful or fraught with fear of harm. It must be remembered at all times when dealing with solunar returns that the Moon's indications are those of eventualities which cause the native to react in ways defined by its relationships in the chart. The house position should be heeded first, inasmuch as the fore-middle-background scheme is basic in any delineation.

The Moon in the Foreground. When the Moon is to the fore, the native is peculiarly susceptible to a naive emotional reaction to every vagrant feeling he experiences. This is an unstable position, from one point of view, as the native often appears to vascillate from one end of the emotional spectrum to the other, making up his mind one day and changing it the next. The reason for this mental dispersion is plainly that his life becomes a stage upon which the scenes and acts change with kaleidoscopic confusion, thereby not allowing him repose and privacy for reflection and careful judgment. Because the Moon represents "feeling," he is brought intimately close to every passing situation—too close, in fact, for him to get a proper perspective on things. He does things without forethought, with a child-like spontaneity of acceptance. This may lead to indulgence of the appetites, dissipation being the result. So eager is he to become "one of the gang," he throws himself into the spirit of things without questioning the advisability of taking another drink, staying up later than he should, or accepting that invitation to aw-come-on-over, etc.

This is especially true of a rising Moon, which seems to give him qualms about daring to be "different" from others. A 1st-house Moon denotes lack of restraint, so that he yields readily to outside temptations, which seem more innumerable and tantalizing than ever during the chart-period in question. He becomes the object of concern or interest to others who invariably get him mixed up in their own affairs. If the Moon is in the 4th house, the native allows these outside complications to get an inroad into his erstwhile most private surroundings (home, den, bedroom, etc.). Of course, the actual nature of these developments depends upon lunar configurations. Should the Moon reside in the 7th house, the native discovers himself wrapped up in activities and associations rather far from his usual base of operations. He is proselytized into participating in partisan causes, finds himself the party-of-the-second-part in some legal or business deal, if not marriage itself (!), or is forced by circumstances to appear in public. He becomes a much-talked-about person in the meantime, as a 7th-house Moon invariably calls the attention of otherwise disinterested people to his affairs. An elevated Moon performs in much the same way, although the attention of outsiders is usually from a higher (social and professional) rank than his own. Things concerning the native are in some way brought under the scrutiny and judgment of superiors (usually his employer) who benefit or demerit him as the case may be.

The Moon in the Middleground. The middleground houses are to be preferred insofar as the Moon's location is concerned, for they refer to those departments of life in which simple satisfaction is more direct, i.e., resources, pleasure, dividends and "dreams." There is not that direct exposure to outside entanglements of the foreground when the Moon is middlegrounded, nor that passive weakness that characterizes the background. The attention is mostly drawn by ramifications of a local nature, such as with reference to income, friends, romance, etc. With Moon in the 2nd house, the aspect-caused complexities occur in the realm of salary, one's natural resources and assets, and physical comforts. The 5th house, on the other hand, emphatically concerns the activities of the libido, the physical attractiveness and adornments, and recreational pursuits. The 8th house denotes one's dependency on others, or the way and extent to which the affairs, goods or demands of others intervene in the native's own life. Therefore, with the Moon there, the native may find himself inextricably involved in issues which call for great concessions to others. He may have to house or support others, or becomes a scapegoat, shouldering blame or burdens not rightfully his own. An 11th-house Moon is excellent, if that Luminary is unafflicted, for it denotes the fulfillment of an ambition, or the opportunity to make one's self seen and heard. It always seems to bring about a state of affairs where the native is required to commit himself, in promise, oath or admission.

The Moon in the Background. Passiveness and exhaustion are tokens of the Moon in background houses. The vitality seems depleted, and the viewpoint is decidedly lax and narrow, as though it required effort to be vivacious. However, a background Moon lessens the danger of wasting effort in worthless ventures, for the native is faced with intensely personal, private matters, and does not have time or the means (other things in the chart permitting) with which to become caught up helplessly in the tide of external activities. The cadent houses, especially the 3rd and 6th, are detrimental to the health, as the resistance to disease is very weak and the recuperative powers are at low ebb. Therefore, the Moon's malefic aspects work for further debilitation. The more favorable aspects involving the backgrounded Moon are trivial in importance, unless the planets concerned are angular.

Lunar Aspects

Naturally, the Moon is so passive by nature, its actual house position, considered alone, is of little consequence. The lunar aspects, however, are of supreme importance in the chart, bespeaking as they do the major eventualities which will befall the native during the sidereal month or year under consideration. Solar aspects, recall, signify acts-of-self, through the function of will. Lunar aspects denote external happenings which cause the native to respond accordingly.

As inferred in the previous chapter, **Sun-Moon** configurations are sign-posts along the highway of life. An opposition of the Lights usually presages that the year or month in question brings the native to a fork in the road, a turning point, or culmination of some sort, wherefrom he is forced to strike out in another direction. The symbolism of the Full Moon itself yields us a clue to its meaning: The native reaches, as it were, a point of greatest expansion or farthest possible outreach, the only movement left being a turnabout or retracement of the steps taken to reach his present position in the scheme of things. Such an opposition, therefore, never fails to alter the scene in some basic, sometimes drastic, manner. Analysis of the general tenor of solar and lunar indications in the chart will reveal just how and why such an innovation will come about. All soli-lunar aspects imply busy-ness. The native often becomes "involved" with people and things ordinarily outside his private little world. His affairs become silhouetted sharply against the broad background of "social relationships," for his connections with other people become of prime importance during the period charted. A conjunction of the Sun and Moon implies such intensive concentration of selfhood with the not-self that conflicts often boil up in the soul, to the native's own undoing. A "combust Moon" is therefore held to be a most adverse influence. Swept along in the tide of life's exigencies, the native, passionately wanting to escape family and social entanglements, is like an ant or bee who never seems to find the chance to relax and regain self-composure.

When the Moon and **Mercury** are configurated, the native is the recipient of offers, important correspondence or telephone calls, and is forced by circumstances to give account of himself, answer questions, and sign his name. Hence, contracts, application blanks, questionnaires and documents command his attention, and he seems at times to be hopelessly trapped in "red tape." Moon-Mercury frequently manifests in his being a candidate, the object of interviews or investigation. People come to him for his autograph and biographic material, and he is a topic of conversation in realms where he is not personally known (cast return charts of persons having been brought into the public limelight by election or contest and see what we mean). Moon-opposition-Mercury suggests a spontaneous arousal of outside interest in the native, whereas the conjunction calls for a forced notoriety such as the native's doing something actively for which publicity is unavoidable. Also part and parcel of Moon-Mercury influences is the necessity for travel, the setting of deadlines which must be met at all costs, and occasions where the native is called upon to speak whether he wishes to do so or not.

The native invariably becomes the target of someone's affection when he is under the ægis of **Moon-Venus** aspects, the conjunction in particular. The opposition indicates gay abandon, stimulation of the erogenous zones of the body under the tender pressure of a romantic opportunity, and temptations aplenty. It was Paracelsus, no less, who said, "The Moon casting a ray to Venus causes the seminal fluid to swell and seek release." The conjunction results in full physical satisfaction, while the opposition, more often than not, represents temptations which appear unexpectedly and cause great tumescence, but which vanish quickly into the mist. The square between Moon and Venus is a splendid social impetus, bringing to the native great popularity and happiness through provocative friendships. The sextiles and trines are most beneficial to the native's all-around social interests, but they lack that forceful sensuous excitement promised by the conjunction, square and opposition. All Moon-Venus angles are auguries of happiness, friendship, social enhancement, and beautification. Music appreciation, singing, dancing and partying are typical outworkings of these most desirable configurations. The native is always convinced that he never felt better in his life!

Moon-Mars aspects, on the other hand, are the reverse of the la-dee-da action of Venus, for they connote strife, irritation, temper and injury. The trines and sextiles usually prevent crises of a tempestuous nature, but do not block entirely the Martian discontent. There is frequently so much work to do during such lunar aspects to Mars, the native becomes so absorbed in the occupations at hand that no ill effects are knowingly felt by him. It is difficult to reach the end of a lunar return period in which the Moon was conjoined, square or opposed to Mars, without having several wounds to lick, or people to get even with, or repair bills to pay. Accidents most frequently take place at this time, and everything seems slated to "go wrong." More often than not, the native is the target of accusations, frame-ups or somebody's revenge. The conjunction, most of all, threatens fisticuffs. The native, angered by the trend in his affairs, deploringly wonders "why they won't leave me alone." Generally, it will be found that Moon-Mars aspects are indicative of inflammation and fever, a poor physical economy, and susceptibility to colds, muscular pains, boils and pustular pimples.

When **Jupiter** and the Moon are in major aspect, the native's worldly standing is bettered, and he has cause to be enthusiastic. Sextiles and trines are financially helpful, but the other majors are the miracle-workers where receipt of large sums or the winning of prizes is in the offing. A candidate for public office can hardly expect election if Moon-Jupiter configurations are lacking in his return charts. Since lunar aspects denote things which happen to, rather than being caused by, the native, Moon conjunct, quartile or opposed to Jupiter are auguries of great honor, elevation, profit and entitlement. Matters connected with money, investments, loans and property rights, require his attention, usually advantageously.

There is little incentive to gain or expansion of worldly interests in charts where the Moon and **Saturn** are in formation, for these denote setbacks, losses, sorrows, and blows to the native's pride which give rise to regrets and grief. The surest token of Moon-conjunct-Saturn is deprivation and disappointment, for the native suffers through loss and denial. Ofttimes, the health is undermined through poor circulation, constipation, rheumatism and worry. Typical Saturnian accidents, toward which there is a definite predilection, are crushing, bruising, bone fractures, falling, and the like. Such things as brain tumors, blood clots and ulcers are sometimes activated when the Moon and Saturn are configurated. Where personal relationships are involved, a bereavement is not unlikely, although the aspects more commonly cause the breaking up of old friendships, being placed at a social disadvantage, and becoming the victim of a theft. Never fail to weigh the potency of any planetary indication against the whole chart-context, for from this one learns the department of life or general locale in which an influence works itself out.

Memorable is the year or month in which the Moon and **Uranus** are in the foreground and connected by aspect. The native finds himself catapulted into experiences heretofore beyond his grasp or even knowledge. Things seem to happen with lightning-like suddenness, catching him unawares. He is thrown in with unusual people or enjoys adventures which open up to him entirely new worlds full of intrigue and enticements. His common reaction, under Moon-Uranus aspects, is, "Look what I've been missing all along!," or, to a newfound companion, "Where have you been all my life?" Uranus connotes excitement and the urge to escape boredom, so that when the Moon releases the valve, the native finds himself the object of truly different, vivifying experiences. The native learns new things which capture his fancy, and sheds caution and discretion, for he discovers the bliss of freedom from convention and a meat-and-potatoes kind of existence.

Should the Moon and **Neptune** be in major aspect, the native is subject to humiliation and puzzlement. The best laid plans of mice and men crumple up in an unsightly heap under the action of Neptune which seems bent upon the frustrating, ridiculing and final failure of every personal motive. The conjunction, in particular, is the most ignominious in effect. The square and opposition point to intrigue and delusion of the native who is exploited and lied to. Circumstances arise which perplex or vampirize him and cause him to feel "cornered," as though some mysterious plot against him was operating. The trine and sextile are not so severe in effect and tend only to keep him in a state of apprehension and misunderstanding. Moon-Neptune aspects in general portend danger from poisonous substances, rancid foods, use of drugs, consumption of liquor and delirium-tremens during the intoxication. The paralytic diseases are Neptunian.

Pressure is brought to bear on the native who is under strong Moon-Pluto influences in the form of critical eventualities which force him to "lay his cards on the table." Aspects of the Moon and Pluto result in such typical upsetting episodes as when the native accidentally bumps into someone on the street to whom he has owed money for many years and cannot this time renege on payment. Or, he is commanded to once and for all make up his mind about something vital to his future and well-being. Swiftness and unerring directness characterize the major happenings of the year and month if Moon and Pluto are in conjunction, square or opposition in the return chart. Note the houses involved in any such formation, for these label the locale where the native may expect nerve-jangling dramatic scenes to transpire.

CHAPTER 5

SOLUNAR INTERPRETATION: THE PLANETS

Mercury

INASMUCH as Mercury is never farther from the Sun, apparently, than 28°, it is usually in the same house held by old Sol, or in one adjacent thereto. This very condition of dependency upon the Sun affords us a keen symbol of Mercury's significance in any chart. Mercury, then, is the "mouthpiece" of the native, in the colloquial sense of the word, being the instrument by which an individual has direct contact with the outside world. Hence, we say Mercury rules speech, "the mind," writing, gesticulation, dexterity, adaptability, and the nervous system. Concretely, Mercury is **social intercourse,** the bridge between the ego and the external universe over which a person sends his thoughts, in the form of words and mannerisms, and receives the communications of others. If Mercury were non-existent, every man would forever be an unintelligible stranger to all other humans, not only eternally "at a loss for words," but wholly unable to understand or make himself understood.

Hence, if Mercury is in the **foreground** of solunar return charts, the communication and adaptive abilities are of front-and-center importance, so that events and trends consonant with Mercury's function take place. Talking, writing, and reading, in all forms but especially for business purposes, keynote the native's affairs. His tongue is glib, his face unusually expressive, and his mind, trigger-quick. With Mercury angular or highlighted, therefore, the year or month in question is characterized by talkativeness, interviewing, gleaning of information, rapid flow of ideas, business dealing and traveling. With Mercury in the **background,** the native feels that he is being ignored by the passing world, for people do not come to him with business or for information, and he is not "called upon" to express his own ideas or voice his opinions. **Middleground** positions of Mercury are of little consequence; Mercury is so "neutral" as to have trite effects even in the foreground, if free of close aspects. While the Sun is "attitude," Mercury may be thought of as "overt activity": this is the ready clue to interpreting Mercurial indications in any return chart.

Mercury-Venus. Only the conjunction and sextile are possible between Mercury and Venus, the former chief in importance. A conjunction usually implies a conversation with a loved one, or a coming to terms with people of whom the native is very fond. It is the perennial index of a proposal or confession of love, especially if in the 7th house. Where this is not plausible, the influence implies intellectual companionship, the "artistic touch," and "travel for pleasure." Strong Mercury-Venus vibrations accompany the urge to write love-letters!

Mercury-Mars. These configurations result inevitably in such unpleasantries as arguments, accusations, slander, libel, and "jumping to conclusions" with unfortunate consequences. For the businessman, it is often a harbinger of trouble with a customer. There is also the ever-present tendency toward accidents during any kind of motion, to wit, traveling, driving, running, and athletics. The native has an excess of nervous energy which he must "blow off" in one way or another. Alcoholism and drug-taking are most often due to a psychological conflict between "cerebrotonia" and "somatotonia," which are basic "components of temperament." Mercury is the most cerebrotonic of planets, Mars the most somatotonic. Hence, Mercury-Mars influences denote escape practices of this sort.

Mercury-Jupiter. Keys to this planetary combination are "commerce" and "big ideas." A very propitious aspect where business and one's income is concerned, a native's fame and fortune (taken relative to his usual status in life) is increased. He is honored for his suggestions and sought out by others for interview. He receives offers and information which make him jubilant. Travel usually enhances his prestige and pocketbook. Success through the mails, newspaper advertising, and by means of interviews or applications, usually are guaranteed by the presence of strong Mercury-Jupiter vibrations.

Mercury-Saturn. Like Mercury-Jupiter, these configurations bear upon a multitude of subjects. Primarily, however, they are indicative of the making of serious mistakes, ofttimes through a faulty memory, which result in losses. They also speak of situations where the native may find himself bound by law or contract to give up rights to or ownership of properties. He learns facts which make him brood. Pessimism, sarcasm, and selfish viewpoints intrude into his life. He "tells people off," writes embittered letters (or receives them—it works both ways), and faces disappointments which cause him to deport himself in a disagreeable manner. The mind may tend to be sluggish, and the speech awkward and hesitant. Slowness and delays in transportation often characterize the period's activities.

Mercury-Uranus. The period scintillates with intellectual thrills, fascinating discoveries, and new inventive ideas, when Mercury and Uranus are in major formation. One's first initiation into the subject of astrology often coincides with a prominent Mercury-Uranus aspect. The native dares to "speak up," despite the consequences for possibly ruffling others, during such periods. The smug religionist may receive intellectual jolts, or the materialist an experience damaging to his whole concept, under such an influence, for Mercury-Uranus is life's stonecutter. This planetary combination bares the truth in bas-relief—a sight often painful to many people. Other feasible interpretations include "a surprise through the mail," and "a challenge to one's intelligence."

Mercury-Neptune. Misrepresentation, fanciful autistic thinking, and frustration of one's plans, are common effects of this influence. The native is duped by strangers, usually, and makes wrong moves and decisions. Promises or commitments made under this impetus end tragically. The native has reason to distrust the truth and sincerity of persons approaching him solicitously. A frequent manifestation of this influence is the stark embarassment one feels when having blurted out the wrong thing to say, under the circumstances. The native under this influence must not only guard his tongue, and turn his ear away from gossip-mongers, but he should ward off a tendency to suspect that the whisperings of others are about himself, or, if they are, that they aren't important enough to get upset over.

Mercury-Pluto. Circumstances cause great nervous tension when Mercury and Pluto are prominently related. The native may be backed up against the wall of convention or written law, and must "fight his way out" of the predicament. Crises arise which tax his patience, force him to "face the music," and declare openly his stand on matters. Under terrific nervous pressure, he may be forced to sign his name, as with regard to a loyalty-oath. This influence is the astrological index of "being given the third degree."

Venus

Venus has sole rulership over matters pertaining to love, marriage, intimacy, friendships, sense stimulants, and beauty. When in the **foreground,** this planet incites romantic interests, erotic experiences, social pleasantries, fine artistry, and gift-bearing as a token of affection. The native finds himself (or herself, as the case may be) pleasantly thrown in with gay groups of people with whom he becomes popular. He has reason to be happy and optimistic, if for no other reason than that he is looking his best and feels unhampered in conversational chit-chat. Venus in the **background,** on the other hand, is inhibitive to his "personality style," and he avoids social mingling through a disinterest in such things. Romance simply does not seem to be his lot in life at this time, so he prefers to be a home-body and is not meticulous about his appearance. As always, however, aspects and zodiacal backdrops are more telling than individual house positions alone.

Venus-Mars. A conjunction of Venus and Mars, especially if in the 7th house, and configurated with the Moon, usually denotes an encounter with one of the "great loves" of one's life. The romantic embers are fanned to conflagration proportions, in some cases. This type of "love" is essentially physical in its origin and survival, unlike the Venus-Moon sort which thrives on imagined, spiritual qualities. Without the absorbent, tenderizing involvement of the Moon, Venus-Mars influences often conduce toward a mixture of love and cruelty. The native may even spurn the affectionate advances of another, unless he accepts those overtures only for what physical delights the opportunity might afford. With carnal appetite having thus been satisfied, his interest in the affair is dropped thoughtlessly, and he hurts the feelings of the other party. Mars is always sadistical, in one way or another, so Venus-Mars configurations infer that the native offends those who are fond of him. The sexual impulse is invariably kindled under this influence, but there is a noticeable lack of sincerity and sympathetic warmth, which defeats congeniality.

Venus-Jupiter. When the two benefics are prominently related by aspect, the native is carried aloft on a magic carpet of enthusiasm. His affairs run harmoniously, he receives gifts, and he bubbles over with carefree exuberance. He is honored by the plaudits of friends, finds himself in more luxuriant surroundings than is ordinarily his tramping-ground, and enjoys general "good luck." Should the Moon be involved in the pattern, he might easily be the winner of a contest or drawing. Venus-Jupiter manifestations may be typified by the jubilance a man, whose salary has been raised, feels as he bursts through the door to embrace his wife while telling her the good news.

Venus-Saturn. Hate or remorse in some way rears its ugly head in the life when Venus is configurated with Saturn. "A woman scorned" is a phrase appropriate to the vibration. The native suffers loss of friends and popularity, and undergoes the most soul-distressing disappointments in his life. The native finds his friendly overtures coldly refused. He has reason to deplore having committed himself in deed or pledge to some person heretofore to his liking. Socially, he may be gripped by acute feelings of inadequacy, made to feel "the poor cousin," "all thumbs," etc. Venus-Saturn detracts from personal attractiveness, by dulling the luster of merry eyes, causing dryness of the hair, and a general impression of weariness in the features. Young people under a return showing this influence strongly are apt to get the feared "stick-in-the-mud" partner, if agreeing to a blind-date—there is a noticeable lack of **any** kind of beauty when Venus-Saturn reigns!

Venus-Uranus. This combination presages unique erotic experiences, particularly of the tabooed kind. The native is faced with and yields to sporadic temptations which result in his discovering new sensuous delights. This influence always reinforces and brings to the surface the homoerotic component in human nature, usually latent or suppressed into the foreconscious mind. He or she has the impulse or finds good reason to renew the wardrobe, "doll up," and "go places and do things." This aspect conduces toward popularity, excitement, and emotional thrills. The native makes changes in his choice of companions, preferring a wholly different scene for the pursuit of pleasures. There is no room for remorse in his otherwise many-sided reel of emotional responses to the things he does or experiences.

Venus-Neptune. Among all the planetary combinations, this is the proverbial "kiss of death," for under its influence, the native is placed in a position of painful embarassment, made a fool of in front of other people, especially those he likes, and is often double-crossed by trusted friends. Venus-Neptune vibrations conduce toward romantic thraldom, of the kind which inspires to ecstasy, and then humiliates. Configurations of these planets give rise to that kind of "hurt inside" which makes us go home alone, somewhat dazed by an unhappy turn of events, and throw ourselves across the bed ungracefully to sob in self-pity. It is a sign of moral weakness, in the conventional sense, for the native's resistance to temptation buckles under him, and he gives in, come what may.

Venus-Pluto. These configurations precipitate climaxes in the emotional life, such as the arrival at a point where a show-down with friends or a romantic partner is called for. Precedents are invariably established in the social life. In the very young, Venus-Pluto often indicates the first tangible erotic experimentation. If Mars and Uranus are prominent in the return chart of young women, with Venus-Pluto to the fore, an initiation into the "facts of life" may be more literal than a mere parental sermon would allow. Several astrologers have reported a prominence of Pluto in such events as the first marriage, the first child, the first freedom a sibling realizes "out on his own," and the like.

Mars

No hiatus is in store for the native with Mars in the **foreground** of his return chart, for this planet always endows an excess of energy which is spent in rigorous work, aggressiveness, and outbursts of temper. Mars angular is always adverse for the health, as it predisposes toward inflammation, common colds, release of accumulated toxins through pimples and boils, and such fulminating painful maladies as appendicitis and hemhorroids. Naturally, there is a tendency toward cuts and nosebleeding. (Destroyed tissue, as from bruises, is a Saturnian indication, primarily.) The fire of life seems fanned to burn more brightly at this time, consuming in the process too much of the vital reserve. Since Mars is "the warrior," the native is in peril of injury through provoked fights, as he is not careful of his speech and attitude, which too often is unpleasant and boisterous. There seems to be a deep-seated yen toward cruelty and bullying. A **background** Mars signifies docility and restraint of the temper. The native in this case lets things ride, is only too glad to shirk work, and neither makes nor accepts challenges where the mettle of character or ability is at stake. A foreground Mars denotes the taking of risks; a background Mars implies reticence. (Surgical operations, on the other hand, do not require a foreground Mars, as Mars in the 6th is just as potent a sign of surgery as a rising Mars.)

Mars-Jupiter. Major configurations of Mars and Jupiter are signs of over-indulgence of the coarser appetites, the squandering of money, and undue excess of generosity. The native usually finds himself holding the bag after spending its valued contents on foolish things, in poor investments, and in behalf of undeserving people who "take him for all he's worth." The normal key-phrase of this planetary combination is "trouble through money"; rest assured that the native will have less at the end of the chart-period than he started with, for this money-to-burn impulse has never resulted profitably for anyone. This pair of planets also inclines toward the acquisition of money or positions of power, through criminal strategy. (It is therefore no surprise that "the Fox," kidnapper Hickman, committed his crime with ransom as the motive, with angular Mars-trine-Jupiter in his prevailing lunar return. His passion for money resulted in a national atrocity.)

Mars-Saturn. No more destructive influence can be found than this planetary combination in major aspect, for it cannot possibly result in good, even when in trine or sextile. "Brute force" is the apt keynote, for it destroys, pillages, and lays waste. Of course, these are the **extreme** effects of Mars-Saturn. In everyday life of ordinary people, this vicious partnership inclines to accidents, paralysis, delays and obstacles, which cause the native to strike out clumsily and blindly in an effort to "save himself and his," or avert possible misfortunes which may threaten. To be sure, there is no such salvation in the offing, so the erstwhile valiant attempt does more harm than good. The best way to thwart this influence—and most adverse influences can be diverted by right action, by the way— is to avoid the throng and possible danger-areas. Cut down on the consumption of spices and such preservatives as salt, for blood-clots most often form under Mars-Saturn impetus. Mars-Saturn is also the "dirty linen" in one's life, so beware of the trouble-maker who might make capital out of your darkest secrets.

Mars-Uranus. Mars, as force, in combination with Uranus, as thrill, poses some pretty interesting possibilities of expression. Among these might be mentioned the impulse toward outlandish mischief, dare-devilish doings, and the like, for the native is moved to attract outside attention by heroic stunts. (Cf. Aviator Lindbergh's pre-flight lunar return for the first take-off point, which shows an angular square of Mars and Uranus.) In his automobile he burns with a desire to push the accelerator to floor-level "to see how fast the old buggy will go," etc. More usually, however, this influence works itself out in great productivity of work, as its keyword is "industry." Primarily a rebellious influence, the native will in all likelihood hustle about tearing out by the roots old interests, old connections with people for whom a sudden dislike is realized, etc. The chart-period during which this combination is prominent will see some radical changes taking place in the native's life, for he uses violence to model things more to his liking, instead of letting evolution do the trick.

Mars-Neptune. This is another of those "killing" combinations, due to its potency for evil-working in the life. Its keywords are "terror" and "betrayal," but bear in mind that these are extremes, and not the common expectancy (or civilization would have wiped itself out long ago!). The native invariably finds himself distraught when a Mars-Neptune configuration is angular in his return chart. He has fear-producing premonitions of disaster. His system reacts violently to any intrusion of drugs or tainted foodstuffs, as this is a very health-debilitating influence. While basically toxic in effect, the combination always indicates the peril of pain or death through fire and fumes. Neurotic trends may evidence themselves in the native's make-up, for his emotional pattern is skewed under this vibration. The native is subject to brutality and cruelty by others, and is tormented by fear of ridicule and public disgrace. Again, these aspects have such a myriad of appropriate meanings, we are stinted from full elucidation of their probable effects beyond this general statement.

Mars-Pluto. Swift meting out of justice is the surest token of strong aspects between Mars and Pluto. Suspense, as tense as a fictional serial chapter-ending, clutches the native's senses sometime during the period covered by the chart. A crisis which calls for the native's taking of the initiative and responsibility is in the offing, for a keyword of Mars-Pluto is "the blame." The combination is essentially criminogenic, and the native may actually perpetrate misdeeds for which retribution follows swiftly and mercilessly.

Jupiter

Jupiter is the planetary herald of fame and fortune, for it is through the prominence and aspects of this planet that all honors, all fulfillments of ambition, and all pecuniary rewards are forthcoming. When Jupiter is in the **foreground**, the native is the happy receiver of money, elevations in rank, titles and prizes, and enjoys general prosperity. But if the Greater Benefic is cadent, in the **background**, the native must be satisfied with his present lot in life and with what he already has, for honors and donors seem to ignore his presence in the world. Aside from these purely "worldly" connotations, Jupiter is the "luck factor" of life, denoting the success of any effort, even the happy end of an erotic quest. The reason why Jupiter is often found in the foreground in cases of illness is not a contradiction of solunar theory, for it refers to the fact of medical care and the attention one receives while bed-ridden. Jupiter is to the fore in pre-demise charts, once in a while. It doubtless pertains, in such cases, to the fact of medication, public sympathy, and even the posthumous eulogies one gets but hardly appreciates at that stage.

Jupiter-Saturn. These configurations are long-term influences in effect, and tend to delay or diminish income. When Jupiter and Saturn are in foreground aspect, any money the native receives will have been worked for strenuously under circumstances which cause him to feel that the effort is not worth-while. People do not enjoy windfalls or win contests when this influence emanates from their charts. It always denotes either reduced income or further financial obligations which prevent any general improvement in the economic status. Various basic keynotes range from "retirement," "indebtedness," and "voluntary self-denial," to "religious awareness."

Jupiter-Uranus. Just the reverse of Jupiter-Saturn influences, these point to sudden windfalls and "runs of luck" which lead to unanticipated rises in the economic level of the native. Sudden honors often befall him, and he not infrequently receives most favorable notices, to his great joy and profit. If he has struggled for some time to make his mark in the world, these configurations will most certainly bring about conditions whereby he may finally make the grade. The keynote of this combination is "success."

Jupiter-Neptune. These aspects conduce toward disillusionment, exploitation, and cheating. The native may find that he has become the victim of a financial swindle, or has been tricked into an agreement or business deal and thereby becomes a "sucker." The influence often causes enthusiasm to soar to sublime heights, only to have the bubble of hope burst pitiably into nothingness.

Jupiter-Pluto. No flights of the imagination are allowed by this planetary combination, which is the harbinger of the end of an old and beginning of a new cycle in the native's relationship to his career, his financial status, and the outside world. (Cf. the speedy coronation of new kings.) It is the marker of crises which make or break the native's reputation, by forcing grave issues out into the light of day, for all to see and judge.

Saturn

Saturn, as a malefic, is essentially destructive, and when it is in the **foreground,** the native's whole well-being is in the balance. The health, first of all, suffers through Saturn's devitalizing, contracting influence, so that there is a definite predisposition toward ailments traditionally ascribed to its rulership. (Add elephantiasis to any such list. This ailment is not Jupiterian as many students are wont, on the spur of the moment, to believe.) Saturn in angular houses may also be expected to curtail the native's social interests and activities, for it places him at a distinct disadvantage, making him subject to adverse criticism by others. It is the harbinger of financial setbacks and losses. Should Saturn reside in the **background,** where its effectiveness for inharmony is reduced almost to nil, the native is not restrained by pressing responsibilities which ordinarily prevent his being able to strike out freely and boldly "into the world to seek a fortune."

Saturn-Uranus. When configurations involving Saturn and Uranus together are in the foreground, even though they are long-term influences with world-wide implications, the native will undergo mental conflicts which cause him to act inconsistently, even foolishly, to his own detriment. Persons responding to this vibration tend to abandon pacific principles, in the hopes of obtaining their objectives by any means, fair or foul. So far as external events are concerned, Saturn-Uranus forces break up old conditions; the native may even find himself living away from his family before the influence has run its course of disrupting the status quo.

Saturn-Neptune. A real throne-toppler, this. Among its paramount keywords is "removal," for Saturn-Neptune surely takes first prize for forcing resignations, abdications, exiles, deportations, and firings from jobs. This combination, in the foreground, more commonly is parasitic in effect, particularly where the health is concerned. It saps the body of its "animal heat," the emotions of their esthetic ardor, and the mind of its quick-wittedness. The native may feel that kind of fatigue which is the forerunner of nervous breakdowns. He becomes petty in his ways of thinking by constant suspicions and jealousies, and frequently may even voice such wishes as that his enemies might die. Saturn-Neptune is a key-producer of neurotic symptoms. An effective keyword is "worry"; the native is wont to "fear the worst" regarding his health, at the first little ache or pain. (A transit of Saturn over radical Neptune, for instance, usually provokes a hypochrondriacal concern in even well-balanced individuals, so that a slight physical indisposition is apprehended as a sure symptom of a dread disease.)

Saturn-Pluto. These are aspects which result in the shouldering of unwanted burdens. They denote worries which lead up to some climax in the life, the nature of which is described by the houses and other aspects, as well as transits to natal planets, involved in the configuration. Psychologically, the native becomes calloused in his attitude, bluntly saying exactly what his sentiments are, viz., instead of invoking heaven's blessing on poor, old Aunt Emma's soul, he declares outright his hope that she sizzles in Hades.

Uranus

When Uranus is in the **foreground,** the life of the native is resplendent with unusual, stimulating developments. It promises sudden changes in the environment, new and fascinating experiences which lead to expansion of the outlook and field of interests, and a colorful existence in general. A **background** Uranus, conversely, is suggestive of a casual, quiet, routine period in which little of great moment is in the offing. Students usually have a difficult time accepting the truth that Uranus is essentially benefic in action and purpose; this is doubtless due to the human trait of preserving the status quo at all costs. Under Uranian influences, too many "drastic, upsetting" incidents happen, leaving the untrained user of astrology with the impression that Uranus could hardly deserve its rank with Jupiter and Venus. Remember that electric lights were literally "forced" upon the people, and that havoc reigned in every community where wealthy faddists dared to purchase one of those gol-dern contraptions called a horseless carriage! Nowadays, just dare to keep a horse around!

Neptune

Just as Uranus works through a kind of magnetic action, Neptune applies a sucking action of some sort. The native feels himself the victim of a merciless Fate when Neptune is in the **foreground,** for this prominence of the malefic tends toward feelings of despair, hopelessness, and "unkind cuts" by others. It seems to him that nothing he tries to do works out to full satisfaction. Neptune angular usually coincides with defeats, withdrawals, and resignations. Neptune in the **background,** however, inures the native against the malicious designs of his rivals and enemies, so that he feels competent and able to stand up for his own rights and interests. Occultly speaking, Neptune is the astral plane, or, more correctly, the quality of astral phenomena. "In it thy Soul will find the blossoms of life, but under every flower a serpent coiled.... stop not the fragrance of its stupefying blossoms to inhale."

Pluto

A **foreground** Pluto promises a lively period, for that planet may be relied upon to establish precedents, dramatically bring to end eras in the life, and just as dramatically draw back the curtain on new. Pluto's effects are swift, sensation-creating, and record-breaking. It denotes "firsts" in the life; the native usually plays the leading role in the drama which transpires. For all its "drive" and nerve-fraying action, Pluto tends the native toward slothfulness, taking the "easy way out," for among Plutonian traits is the desire to shirk obligations, not play by the rules, or hold up one's own end of the bargain, etc. From this fact it is apparent that Pluto's extremes include those of ambition and complete lethargy. Pluto also is prominent with regard to freak accidents, "miracles," and inexplicable phenomena, such as "accidentally" running across an old friend on a street hundreds of miles away from the scene of your previous acquaintanceship. Such "fateful" happenings (they are more frequent in a lifetime than pure chance would allow) seem always to take place under prominent Plutonian influences.

CHAPTER 6

SOLUNAR RETURNS IN ACTION

UP TO THE TIME of the introduction—or rather reinstatement—of sidereal astrology, there was in currency no really satisfactory technique for predicting the eventuality of "the thousand natural shocks which flesh is heir to" with any consistent accuracy. Where outright acts-of-self were concerned, the standard progressed horoscope proved itself extremely trustworthy. Still, we students of astrology were often disappointed, even perturbed, that many of life's most climacteric mishaps or windfalls were strangely without proper indications of **comparable** power in the progressed horoscope for the time of the event.

"Transits," by themselves, were equally inconsistent, although were usually made to satisfy the case. Then, previous "New Moon degrees" were frequently brought to bear with sporadic success, but none too convincingly. Once in a while, the **causa formales** was thought to be found in a solar revolution or lunar return chart, cast in terms of the tropical zodiac. Again, with only scattered and questional evidence favoring the validity of the method. Key Cycles and Birth Diurnal Figures were employed here and there among astrological students, all with admittedly meager results. To put it bluntly, modern astrology, with its dozens of systems, was becoming more and more like the Bible—you can prove anything by the Good Book. All this while the star-spangled backdrop of the sky overhead held the answer long sought by modern astrologers.

The little child who ran happily across the street to join her playmates, and was killed instantly by a passing auto, was a victim of an accident unshown by her progressed chart. The businessman enroute to New York by air whose body was found amid the wreckage of a plane atop a mountain was not killed by any natal "anareta" or progressed aspect. What, then, is the rationale of violent death, if we fail to find "progressions" genuinely suggestive of violent death? While we may hasten to our ephemeris and other regalia, shortly afterward exclaiming, "Aha!" to learn that the plane took off at an ominous time, we have not found the reason for the deaths of the individual passengers. In most cases, we are prevented by circumstances from obtaining the birth data of such individuals in order to make a study of this troubling problem. But, we do know that, without fail, the solunar returns of those ill-fated passengers, or that little girl, show plainly the disastrous possibilities haunting that period in their lives in which the mishaps occurred. It is because of the consistent faithfulness of the solunar returns, constellation-wise, that we make bold to recommend their constant use in the lives of everybody devoted to astrology, professionally or otherwise.

The Bitter and the Sweet

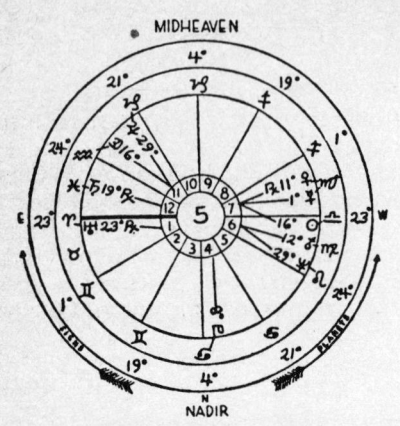

Lunar Return (Male) Self-Discovery

To illustrate the lucidity with which lunar returns preview major events in the life, we present here a series of four charts for different types of developments which over the years engulfed a young man of our acquaintance. The first example is the lunar return preceding his first overt sexual experience, culminating in orgasm which, through both ignorance and innocence, he did not expect. Such an event is vastly important in anybody's life, especially from the psychological standpoint; we cite such an example here without squeamishness because it so well illustrates what we have said about planetary influence. Now, the youth in question had never been given a morsel of "sex education" by either his parents or teachers. Naturally, the impact of the theretofore unsuspected power innate in his own body was overwhelming, even startling.

Notice in Figure 5, the ascendancy of the "thrill planet" Uranus, and the angularity of Venus, Mercury, the Sun and Pluto. Uranus exactly conjunct the Ascendant promised that something unusual, thrilling, startling, would happen to the native during the 27 days following. Uranus in the 1st house always denotes the "thrill of discovery;" the Sun in opposition to Uranus guaranteed that it would be a "self-discovery." Venus, in the constellation Scorpio which relates to the genitalia, is sextile Mars, trine Pluto and square the Moon —ample testimony that this was going to be the month in which our gossoon would discover the pleasures of erotic excitement. Pluto, conjunct the Nadir, is the surest indication of a "first," or unprecedented climax in the private life. This was plainly a turning-point in his existence. Notice also the cadency of the malefics, Mars, Saturn and Neptune—the youth was not adversely affected by the experience as are many who suffer remorse and misgivings untold for having tasted what they were falsely told is the most forbidden of fruits. Striking to the observer is the placement of the Moon and Jupiter in the 11th house—the fulfillment of a fond hope, a vague dream come true, the finding of a sympathetic friend.... The Moon and Sun are trine: the experience was mutually shared, not clumsily but with that natural ease and reciprocity so characteristic of soli-lunar configurations. The Sun, being conjunct the 7th cusp, implies the surrender of individuality to another in a natural union instigated by desire.

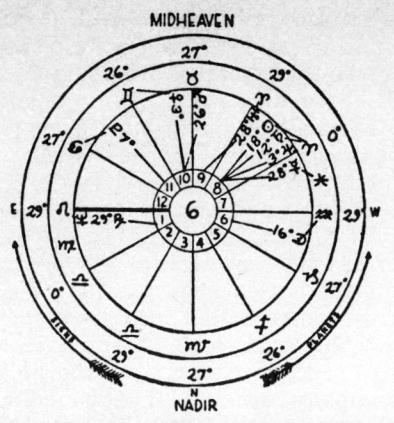

Lunar Return (Male) A Medical Fraud

This potent experience having become part of the young man's past, we find him at a later date the victim of a malicious medical fraud. Figure 6 is his lunar return for that most unusual month when our native visited a doctor to seek a remedy for a minor but annoying skin rash which afflicted his hands and arms. After impressive "tests" were made by that apparently concerned, proficient medico, he was sobrely told that he was the victim of a social disease. What soul agonies our friend underwent in the three weeks following that diagnosis, during which time he received several injections intended for its cure, at a costly fee. Were it not for the suspicions of his family, he might have gone for many months taking this "cure." Through the goading of his family, he went to another doctor who subjected him to the standard examination and pronounced him completely free of any such infection. The rash, it turned out, was a simple fungus which might have been picked up anywhere. An official investigation of the first doctor proved that he had been perpetrating a medical racket involving several duped patients who came to him with minor ailments and were told that they were socially diseased.

The entire experience took place during the span of the one lunar return chart here shown. Any astrologer could immediately have suspected that the native would be **victimized** (always the omen of Neptune) during the sidereal month, for Neptune is exactly on the Ascendant squared by Mars at the Midheaven. Surely, this signifies not only victimization, fraud, and the soul-agony which accompanies realization of serious disease, but also the needle-injections (Mars) of drugs (Neptune) into the body (Ascendant) by a superior (professional, titled doctor, 10th house). The conjunction of Sol and Saturn in the 8th house definitely implies the negation and dread which swamped the man, still very young. From these planetary circumstances alone, an astrologer might have drawn the direst of conclusions. But hold it! The other foreground body is Venus, in exact sextile with 8th-house Jupiter. This promises that the period in question would not be without its blessings, that a happy ending was in store for our distraught native. True to form, the sidereal month ended on a most happy note. Incidentally, the progressed chart of this man did not even remotely imply any such eventuality.

A few years later still, we find our friend a victim of another form of malicious intent. Working for a huge firm in which he had been

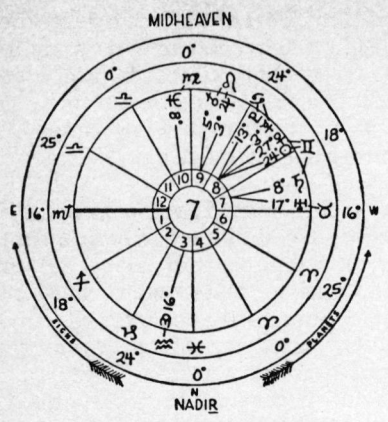

Lunar Return (Male)
Discharge from Job

extraordinarily successful, winning several promotions in the interim, our native was suddenly discharged as an incompetent. He had done nothing to merit such treatment at the hands of his immediate superior, whom he was supposed to replace at some future promotion. Later discovering the real reason for his removal, he learned that his office rivals, marshalled into a conspiracy by that jealous supervisor, had succeeded in convincing high company officials that his employment with them should be terminated.

What does the lunar return (Figure 7) preceding this sudden dismissal show? Neptune in the 10th house in partile square with Saturn in the 7th. Could anything be plainer than such a foreground configuration? We find malicious (square) scheming (Neptune) superior (10th) and rivals (7th) bringing about the loss (Saturn) of a job in a corporation office (7th). The native took this blow to his pride philosophically (Sun conjunct Venus in 8th), and immediately discovered a job much more to his liking, as an advertising agent. This new job is shown by the square of the Moon and Uranus which holds the 7th cusp. He recalls that the most noteworthy element of the whole period was the rapidity with which such changes took place.

Several months following this episode, he met "the ideal girl," immediately fell in love with her (a mutual love-at-first-sight it was) and married her less than two weeks after their first, electric meeting. He had never known such blissful happiness as this single month afforded him. A glance at the preceding lunar return chart (Figure 8) substantiates the fact that his enthusiasm was not exaggerated. The Moon is conjunct Venus in the 4th house: and love did come home to roost! The suddenness of the thrilling experience is shown clearly by the partile square of the Moon to Uranus in the 7th house.

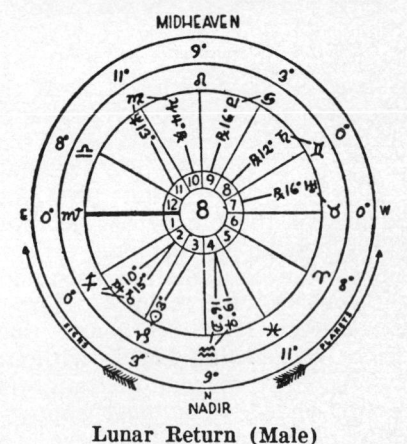

Lunar Return (Male)
Sudden Marriage

None of the malefics are in the

foreground of this chart, while the three benefics are all angular, for Jupiter is in the 10th (trined by the Sun). So we see how amazingly clear the lunar return charts for this man have shown the major happenings of his life with a transparency no other astrological technique has approached. The bitter and the sweet of life are invariably foreshown by the solunar returns.

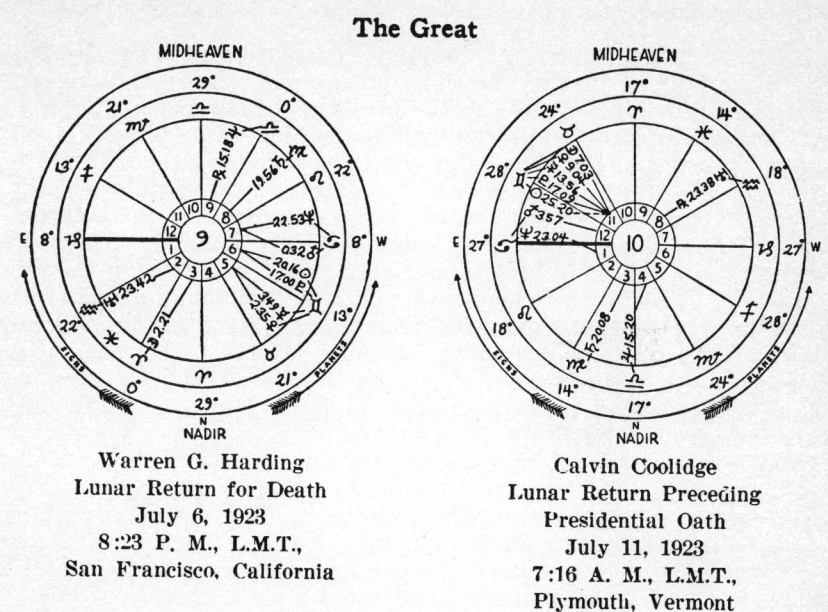

The Great

Warren G. Harding
Lunar Return for Death
July 6, 1923
8:23 P. M., L.M.T.,
San Francisco, California

Calvin Coolidge
Lunar Return Preceding
Presidential Oath
July 11, 1923
7:16 A. M., L.M.T.,
Plymouth, Vermont

In early August of 1923, the wires from San Francisco flashed across the United States the regretful news that their President, Warren G. Harding, had died of ptomaine poisoning in that city, having been hastened there from Alaska which he had been touring officially. Only a few hours later, a proud but noisy motor car jostled its way through the midnight countryside of quaint Vermont to relay the news to Vice President Calvin Coolidge. Blurry from interrupted sleep, Mr. Coolidge yawned, "Well, I guess I'd better get up." There, before dawn broke, old John Coolidge, notary public, administered to his famous son the presidential oath of office, by kerosene lamplight.

Scan the two lunar return charts given here (Figures 9 and 10), noticing the interlocking significance of Harding's and Coolidge's indications for this historic development. Harding's return is typical of demise from natural causes, what with both the Sun and Moon in cadent houses, bespeaking the reason for his inability to throw off the poisons pervading his system. The Sun is conjunct Pluto in the 6th house, ample testimony that Pluto is connected with poisoning.*

---

* Page 47, "Astrological Chats," by Llewellyn George.

Only two planets, Mars and Neptune, "the killers," are in the foreground, holding the 7th house. The background Moon is closely square to Mars, implying the drastically high fever which brought the crisis of demise. Particularly inimical to the health is the close square (within 0°20′) between the background Sun and 8th-house Saturn. No benefics are in the foreground to help offset the glaringly malevolent indications of death.

A most casual glimpse of Coolidge's current chart is equally telling. Here we find Jupiter, planet of honors and rises in station, conjunct the I. C.—his elevation to the presidency took place in his own rural home. Jupiter's wide trine to Uranus hints of a windfall, unexpected honors, and the like. But most impressive is the stellium of five planets in the 11th house, which pertains to the taking of oaths, the coming true of long-felt dreams, congratulatory events, the attention of a vast audience, etc. (Calvin suddenly found he had more friends than a whole White House staff could handle at maximum turn-over.) The Moon's close conjunction with Venus in the 11th is the surest augury that the native becomes an object of affection, admiration, and friendly overtures. Honors always befall the native with aspects to Jupiter, and we find the entire stellium of 11th-house bodies centralizing a trine to angular Jupiter. Mars and Saturn are in the background, but Neptune is astride the Ascendant. The native, therefore, while jubilant that he had become Number One U. S. A., was jittery at the prospect, was unable to think clearly in the swarm of activities and engagements which buzzed through his every waking moment in the days and weeks following Harding's death. Might it also not refer to that now-famous scene that transpired on that fateful night when kerosene lamplight illuminated a most epochal ceremony in the chronicles of American history?

And the Small

Our next exemplary case is that of the death of an 8-year old child (sex not stated by the source of our data, for whom we begrudgingly apologize) in a fire which destroyed its parents' home. The event well illustrates the amazing effectiveness of sidereal solunar returns, in addition to proving the importance of transits to radix positions—something we have left untouched so far in this treatise. Transits are most effective at the moment of lunar return, rather than at partile relationship to natal planets. In actual fieldwork with solunar charts, it is advisable at all times to note the aspective relationships of the planets in the return figure to those of the radix. Also extremely important is the use of the **locality chart**,* especially its angles, with regard to planetary transits. We believe that it will be found by all who consider the matter that transits over the natal

---
* Full details on the equation of the birthchart to other localities are covered in Part V of Llewellyn George's master textbook, "A TO Z HOROSCOPE MAKER AND DELINEATOR."

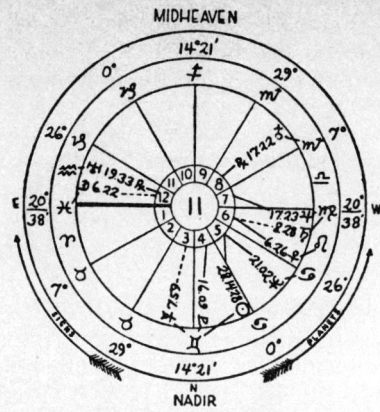

Nativity of Child
Killed by Fire in Home
July 14, 1922
11:06 P. M., L.M.T.,
Oakland, California

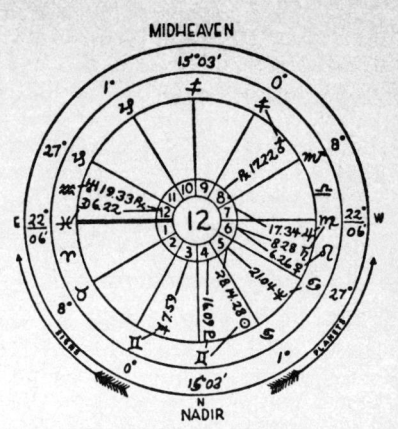

Nativity of Child
Equated to Locality
Sacramento, California

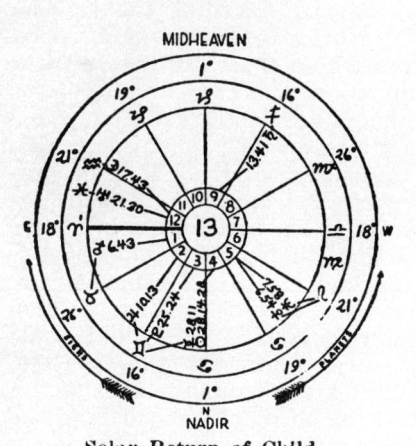

Solar Return of Child
Preceding Death by Fire
July 15, 1930
0:17 A. M., L.M.T.,
Sacramento, California

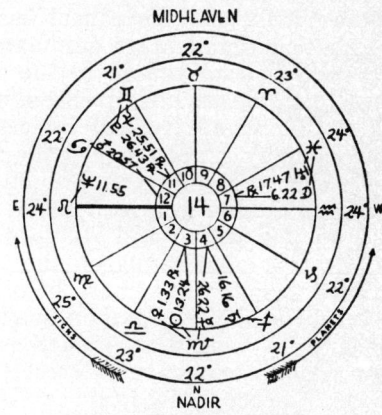

Lunar Return of Child
Preceding Death by Fire
November 30, 1930
0:25 A. M., L.M.T.,
Sacramento, California

angles (Ascendant, Midheaven, Descendant and Nadir) are not felt strongly by a native unless he or she is in the vicinity of the birthplace. We have abundant data to prove that transits to the angles of the locality chart are those most effectual. For instance, a person born in Detroit yet residing in Phoenix will feel the effects of Mars in transit over the Ascendant of his **birthchart equated to Phoenix,**

rather than to transits of Mars over the original (Detroit) cusps. Much more auspicious is a transit of Jupiter through the 10th house of one's locality chart than that of the nativity, etc. An individual fares more fortunately in geographic locations where the benefic planets in his radix are angular and where the malefic planets are cadent. Many astrologers are now highly skilled in the art of selecting more propitious localities for people who have experienced frustration or failure at their usual places of residence. Application of such techniques should become part of the regular service of all astrological practitioners.

The case at hand does not represent a far enough removal of the native from the place of his birth to warrant our drawing any outright conclusions regarding the virtue or viciousness of the slight change of cusps which took place. We include the locality chart with the birthchart for whatever comparison they might afford together. The child in question was born in Oakland, California, and moved to Sacramento where it met its untimely death by fire and suffocation.

Some hint of the forthcoming tragic end is yielded by the nativity: Mars in the 8th house in trine to Neptune and square Uranus. However, it is to the solar and lunar returns preceding the accident that we must look for causal factors. Notice in Figure 13, its solar return, that rising Mars dominates the whole chart, throwing in the process a baleful square to the conjunction of Venus and Neptune. The Moon, meanwhile, is within a few minutes partile square of radix Mars. These are typical indices of death by fire. Saturn, too, is prominent by aspect even while in the background, for it is dangerously near the child's radical Midheaven, and opposed to birthchart Pluto. Pluto is not without its connotations, being in conjunction with conjoined Sun and Mercury near the Nadir. Also impressive is the electrifying Uranus on the radical and locality Ascendant. An astrologer with this chart before him would quickly surmise that sometime in the twelve months to follow its birthday, the child would encounter a most dire, sudden eventuality. Naturally, the alert student would commence to erect the child's forthcoming lunar return charts in order to ascertain for which sidereal month ahead Fate had deigned an appropriate mishap. "Forewarned is forearmed" is an old and very, very true adage; through advance knowledge by astrology we are able to take preventive measures against disasters. It would have been easy to save this little life by knowing beforehand, through these charts, what the threatening probabilities were. Unfortunately, even the most productive, thoughtful astrological student could not possibly keep diligent watchfulness of the indications for each and every person, friend, client or relative within his ken. ("Every man his own astrologer" should become a slogan of every astrological society!)

Inasmuch as Mars, coupled with Neptune by quadrature aspect, was the significator of the disaster, according to the solar return, something similar is to be expected in the lunar return. What do we find in the lunar figure (14) but Mars within 0°05' conjunction with the sibling's natal Neptune! This surely was the cue! Death by fire (Mars) and suffocation (smoke, Neptune). However, because Mars is in the background, we must still not assume that this lunar month was the actuator of previous indications. Uranus is the only foreground benefic, but it is malevolently aspected, a trine by Mars and a close square with Saturn in the 4th house. Uranus, remember, is still conjunct the natal Ascendant.

The crux of the matter is the angular Saturn's opposition to radix Pluto (within 0°07') while straddling the radix Midheaven (more nearly partile to the locality M. C.). Hence, that the parents' home was destroyed is shown in several ways. The youngster was old enough to have saved itself during the conflagration, but it had quickly succumbed to the smoke and fumes billowing into its bedroom (Neptune rising into the 12th house which rules the bedroom, according to old authorities). The cadent Sun's close square with rising Neptune implies some such weakness and susceptibility to gases, but more pre-eminently it scatters the wits, strikes panic into the heart, and generally breaks down the composure. Sun-Neptune aspects are hypnotic in action.

Hence, the chart-indications worked out with extraordinary clearness. It is overwhelmingly significant that, while the transits to radix planets would have been nearly identical, without referring them to any chart frame-of-reference, it is only in the sidereal zodiac that it is possible for **house** positions to be so appropriate. (Solunar returns based on the tropical zodiac are widely divergent from those drawn for sidereal-zodiac positions.)

Death Sentence

In any American court, it is impossible to try a man for murder in the absence of the body of the victim. Yet, the notorious French "Bluebeard," Henri Desire Landru, murderer of eleven, was tried on purely circumstantial evidence, because the bodies of the eleven murderees were never found. Arrested in Paris on April 12th, 1919, when police authorities were satisfied that they had their bloodthirsty culprit, despite the lack of certain proof of his guilt, Landru was brought to trial on November 7th, 1921. During the three-week-long session, in which his fate was being decided by a bevy of jurors, the transitting Moon returned to the place among the stars which it held at his birth. Hence, had we known his birth data before the trial, we could clearly have anticipated what the jury's verdict would be. It is important in this connection to remember that the court was almost completely without a case resting on factual evidence. The prosecution's success or failure depended on the weight of circumstances.

The accompanying figure (15) is Landru's lunar return which occurred six days prior to the verdict. In company with Jupiter in

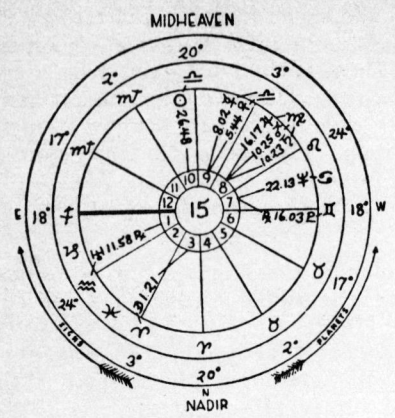

Landru's Lunar Return
Preceding Death Sentence
November 13, 1921
11:18 A. M., L.M.T..
Paris, France

the 8th house, are Mars and Saturn in conjunction by only 0°02′ —judicial death-sentence. The Sun in the 10th house signified the position of the defendant himself: at the mercy of his peers. The Sun squares Neptune in the 7th—a foreground configuration invariably associated with "the jitters" and soul-agony always accompanying one coming face-to-face with the prospect of his own dying. Uranus in the 1st house, trined by background Mercury and Venus, doubtless gave rise to continually renewed hopes that exoneration would follow as the result of the favorable "character-reference" testimony provided by several female witnesses in his behalf. Landru had quite a way with the ladies. In fact, this was the secret of his success as a wholesale slaughterer. Even while on trial for his life, many women who had been in romantic thraldom to him, refused to believe that such a desirable paramour could be guilty of such nasty doings. His winning personality did not fool the court, however, and Landru only succeeded in deluding himself (Sun-square-Neptune). That underneath his suave demeanor his nerves were wracked to the breaking point is evidenced by Pluto on the 7th-house cusp. Pluto's foreground position also provided that sensationalism which characterizes any controversial murder trial, but especially this one.

It is interesting to note that Neptune is within 0°22′ of Landru's radix Mars, bespeaking the indignity which sentencing, not to mention execution, induces. The most prominent feature of Landru's birthchart (April 12, 1869, 6:12 A. M., L. M. T., Paris) is the grand trine of Mars in 24° ♋ 51′, Saturn in 24° ♏ 54′, and Neptune in 25° ♓ 13′, a complete vicious circle of the three planetary "killers." Students convinced that "all trines are good, etc." will have to tread lightly among such choice horoscopic eggs as this! How interesting it is that the lethal end of his nefarious lifetime should be marked by the arrival of transitting Neptune to the place of his radical Mars. Incidentally, this is an excellent chance to compare differences in the effects of a given transit-combination. Mars traversed natal Neptune when the little child discussed a page or two back was burned to death. Landru was beheaded when Neptune crossed his natal Mars In the one case, the death was purely accidental in that the native did not provoke the circumstances. In Landru's case, his own misdeeds created the situation whereby he was forced to lay his own head under

— 66 —

the guillotine blade. From this we deduce that an encounter with stark terror is unexpected and shortlived under Mars-over-Neptune, but anticipated and prolonged under the much slower Neptune-over-Mars transit. Less fateful persons who undergo the latter transit are often heard to wail, "I'm being tortured!" or "I don't know how long I can stand for it!" Referring most of the time to marital or sexual anxieties.

The Winnah!

Stocky Jack Dempsey, though long retired from the boxing ring, will always stand out brightly among the greater lights of the sports world. The story of his rise to fame, and continued popularity despite loss of the title which first glorified his pugilistic skill, is one of those many faceted tales which Americans love to recall and discuss in tones and gestures of intimate familiarity. The astrological background of his boxing career is no less interesting, to us, anyway. Born at 5:24 a. m., L.M.T., in Manassa, Colorado, on June 24th, 1895, Jack Dempsey won the title of World's Heavyweight Boxing Champion in Toledo, Ohio, when Jess Willard, groggy from a last-moment knockout in the 3rd round, failed to answer the 4th bell. The Dempsey-Willard fight took place on July 4th, 1919. Let us see what the solunar returns preceding this bout presaged for the young man from the Rocky Mountains.

We selected Dempsey's charts for presentation here because they offer us some highly interesting tokens of rise-and-fall of a very unique sort. Here, the attainment of honor and acclaim was not bestowed in the usual sense of citation or windfall, for it must needs have been won by physical embattlement—a contest in which "the better man" was to emerge victorious. Therefore, we would expect the gain to be more **Solar** than **Jupiterian***—the Conqueror rather than the Potentate is the central figure. We would also anticipate the pre-eminence of Mars and the diminution of Venus, the former for the show of necessary prowess and the latter for the minimizing of finesse and passive consideration of the other fellow.

Figures 16 and 17 are the solar and lunar returns preceding Dempsey's achievement of the championship. A native of the constellation Gemini, Jack truly carries on the tradition of the athletic Twins of mythology. You will notice, in this connection, the highlighted importance of Mercury, planetary patron of the Geminian starfield. A champion boxer must be brimful of Mercurial quick-wittedness and agility, for hulking strength alone could never make a "champeen." Notice in the solar figure that the warrior Mars is in highest elevation, sans debilitative aspects, which is the classical token of the conquering fighter. The Moon, exalted by sign and position, is in quadrature with Uranus, indicating sudden gain, the

---
* **Jovian** is an academically correct and preferred adjective for use with regard to Jupiter's associations.

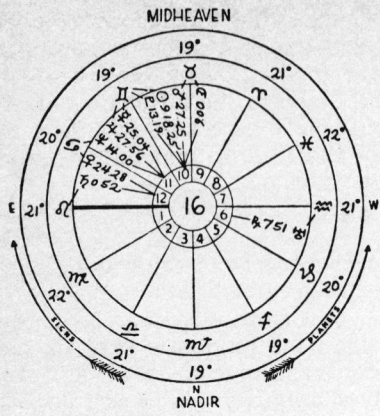

Jack Dempsey's Solar Return
Preceding Win of World
Championship Title.
June 25, 1919
10:33 A. M., L.M.T.,
Toledo, Ohio

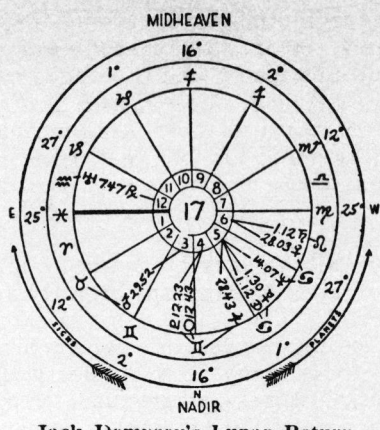

Jack Dempsey's Lunar Return
Preceding Win of World
Championship Title.
June 29, 1919
0:17 A. M., L.M.T.,
Toledo, Ohio

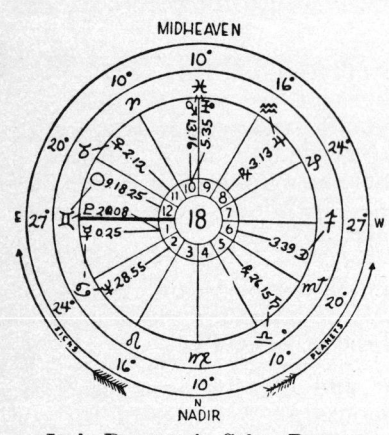

Jack Dempsey's Solar Return
Preceding Loss of Title.
June 25, 1926
6:02 A. M., L.M.T.,
Philadelphia, Pennsylvania

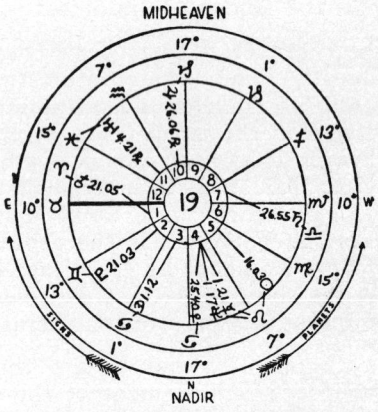

Jack's Dempsey's Lunar Return
Preceding Loss of Title.
September 2, 1926
10:06 P. M., L.M.T.,
Philadelphia, Pennsylvania

brevity of the boxing match, which was only three rounds long, and ebullient audience support. When the Lights are elevated, the native is invariably thrown into the public spotlight and put to the test, as it were, having to show the world "the stuff he's made of."

Most significant is the Sun-Pluto conjunction in the 10th house which promised that this would be a most sensational year, with the native himself the star attraction of nerve-wracking developments. What is more befitting such a configuration than the life of a pugilist skyrocketed to fame as a world's champion? Surely, with the possible exception of a horserace, nothing of a public spectacle is more intensively fraying to the nerves of both participant and spectators than a title-at-stake boxing event. Also in favor of the native's personal ability, as an outreaching act-of-self, is the Sun's trine to Uranus. Hardly needing mention is that Leo, the Sun-patronized constellation, rises in the return chart, its ruler being in the 10th. Especially auspicious, so far as the nature of the native's goal is concerned, is the cadency of the planets Venus and Saturn, within orb of conjunction in the 12th house. Had Venus been in the foreground, Jack might have weakened his advantage through that type of "good sportsmanship" which is bad business so far as the fortunes of a fighter are concerned, in that too great consideration, coupled with a hesitation to hurt the opponent, would have reduced his effectiveness as a hard-hitter. Saturn, in the foreground, would have slowed down his reflexes, and otherwise is an adverse influence for any kind of worldly honor. Mercury and Jupiter are conjunct in the 11th, true-to-form testimony of a dream of honor come true, the newspaper publicity accorded him (the 11th house is anybody's "audience"), and the financial rewards which this Mercury-ruled native arrived at as the fulfillment of his fondest hopes.

The pertinent lunar return chart for this historic fight is no less vivid in its evidences of success, for the Sun-Pluto conjunction, so crucial in the solar return, is within 0°20′ partile at the Nadir. It is not without grounds that a modern keyword for Pluto has become "**coercion**," coined first, I believe, by Elbert Benjamine, after study of apparent Plutonian effects. Furthermore, since Sun-Pluto is the most out-lawful of planetary combinations, it is fascinating that Mr. Dempsey, as well as any other man in modern society, could not **legally** have fought another man, outside the ring, with impunity. It follows that professional pugilism is a wonderful vicarious outlet for persons in whom the disdain for law and suppression is so great as to cause psychological conflicts which might easily resolve into criminalism.

The next most catching feature in the chart is the triple conjunction of Jupiter, the Moon, and Mercury, at the 5th cusp. This clearly reveals that the sidereal month in question was **the** period out of a possible thirteen in which the auguries of the solar return should come to fruition. The plummeting into public view, a life bubbling over with activities, publicity, financial reward, social engagements, considerable travel and autograph-signing, are all indicated by this auspicious configuration. Worth recalling, too, is that the 5th house has much to do with staged sporting events and holiday celebration (the fight took place on the jubilant Fourth of July as a highlight of the holiday festivities and goings-on). As in the solar return, the conjunction of Venus and Saturn is again in the background. Mars cadent was assurance that the "health" of the native would not be impeded by blood-letting injuries. Mr. Dempsey came out of the fight a nearly unscathed victor.

For more than seven years following that day when Jack wrested from Jess Willard the heavyweight title, he fought regularly, each time defending his coveted prize. Then, on September 23rd, 1926, a decision of the judges awarded the championship to Gene Tunney, his challenger in that controversial debacle held in Philadelphia. A year later, Jack contended for a retrieve of his title, but again, after another 10-round session, the decision was in Tunney's favor. Naturally, since Jack Dempsey's rise to glory was so plainly supported by his solunar returns to begin with, we are eager to analyze the returns which preceded that first tussle with Tunney.

Figure 18 is Dempsey's solar return for the unfortunate turn in the tide of his affairs. In it, the opposing Sun and Moon are cadent. Hence, this background Full Moon suggested that Jack had arrived at the pinnacle of success. It speaks clearly of much publicity, congratulatory attention, and what-have-you in the way of soli-lunar influences, but it more plainly is the debilitator of the vitality, the dulling of the sensory faculties, etc. That his bully strength was not impaired is attested to by the position of Mars in the Midheaven, square the Sun, but such a form of energy is more blind and reckless than strategic and calculated. Pluto rising also shows considerable blind force, inasmuch as Mars is square that dramatic, coercive, never-say-die planet. The Sun is trine Jupiter, but this is a weakening influence, where pugilism is concerned. Rising Mercury's trine to Uranus is also not so desirable an index where pugilism is involved, by itself considered, for it shows a little too much mental activity in the form of "trying something new," remembering rules, thinking about the stakes a little too excitedly, etc., to the detriment of his performance in the ring. Jack should have relied upon brute strength and experience to have won this fight; an old dog usually bungles new tricks. Had Mercury been square elevated Uranus, the acuity of thought and agility of style which that planetary combination always gives might have paid better dividends where the judge's opinions counted.

The box-office intake was record-smashing; and, win or lose, Jack's share in the proceeds was enormous. Notice the middleground square of Venus and Jupiter—an indication not only of great popularity with the public regardless of the outcome, but of immense income as well. But, a conjunction of Mars and Uranus at the Midheaven, square the weak 12th-house Sun and weak 6th-house Moon, spelled defeat in battle. Jack's standing in the world changed drastically, under the action of his superiors, who, incidentally, must have been convinced that a "change" (Uranus) was in the offing. Saturn in the 5th house, square Neptune, was adverse to his athletic interests. The student will recall that the primary meaning of Saturn-Neptune aspects is that of removal, lowering of status, loss of worldly position, etc.

Finally, the lunar return preceding his defeat is extraordinarily telling. It reveals at a glance the downward plunge of prestige and rank. This figure (19) has technical interest which, if context were permitting, we would dwell upon at length for the enlightenment of students who probably have pondered the question of **orbs** for the angles. Notice that Mars appears to be 19° above the eastern horizon, yet we have indicated a conjunction with the Ascendant which implies a 1st-house reading. But notice also that the 12th house, due to the obliquity of the ecliptic at this time and latitude, is 55° of longitude in width. A simple calculation proves that Mars is actually **less than 7° in altitude** above the eastern horizon; therefore, it most certainly is within orb of conjunction the Ascendant. Saturn, appearing to be a full 13° down into the 6th house, is actually **less than 4° under the western horizon,** and therefore must be considered as conjunct the Descendant.*

In Dempsey's final lunar return, we find a rare planetary configuration crucifying the chart: a gigantic Grand Cross of Mars, Venus,

---

* Basing this conclusion on altitude alone, however, is not a fully satisfactory solution to the problem, it being increasingly unsatisfactory as the geographic latitude increases. The correct way to determine a planet's "propinquity to an angle" is to compute what zodiacal degree is on the Ascendant or Descendant when the planet itself is exactly on the eastern or western horizon, respectively. This is accomplished through the use of a Table of Ascensional Differences, knowing the planet's Right Ascension and Declination.

A. To determine what ecliptic degree is rising when a planet is exactly on the **eastern** horizon:

1. If the planet's Declination is **North,** add 90° to the Ascensional Difference, and subtract this sum from the planet's Right Ascension. The difference is the R. A. of the M. C. when the planet is exactly on the eastern horizon.
2. If the planet's Declination is **South,** subtract its A. D. from 90°, and then subtract this difference from the planet's R. A. The difference is the R. A. M. C. when the planet is exactly on the eastern horizon.

B. To determine what ecliptic degree is setting when a planet is exactly on the **western** horizon:

1. If the planet's Declination is **North,** add 90° and its A. D. to its R. A. The sum gives the R. A. M. C. when the planet is exactly on the western horizon.
2. If the planet's Declination is **South,** subtract its A. D. from 90°, and add this difference to its R. A. The sum gives the R. A. M. C. when the planet is exactly on the western horizon.

C. Enter a Table of Houses for the necessary latitude, and find what zodiacal degree is on the Ascendant or Descendant for the R. A. M. C. found in the way described. The difference between this degree and the planet's actual longitude tells its "propinquity to the angle" in question. If it is less than 10°, consider the planet within orb of conjunction the cusp.

Saturn and Jupiter on the angles, in cardinal constellations, with Neptune close enough to one corner of this pattern to be an added malevolence. This whole situation is another reason why we wished to present Dempsey's charts in this series, for the lunar return is one of those "catch-questions" which would perhaps delude less wary and experienced students. The close foreground opposition of Venus and Jupiter is ordinarily (and always, actually) a marvelous indication of gain and worldly credit. It was definitely that in Dempsey's case, for the influence would work itself out appropriately despite the afflictions, in netting for him vast riches, unprecedented publicity and widespread adulation by boxing fans the world over. But that he was to be defeated and deprived of his title is surely shown by the nearly-partile square to Venus and Jupiter of Saturn, aided and abetted by further squares of Mars. Foreground Neptune is square foreground Saturn and in opposition to foreground Jupiter, as well as within 0°04′ conjunction Dempsey's patron, angular Mercury. The Leo Sun in the 5th house is trine Mars, calling attention to a sportive "battle royal," but this was more of a self-effacing kind of influence than an advantage. The Moon is again cadent, its trine with Uranus in the 11th thereby being rendered even weaker. All in all, it is a chart of defeat, of a brilliant career brought upsettingly to a close. Dempsey could rest comfortably on his record-breaking laurels, however, for that Venus-Jupiter relationship prevented any possible disgrace or loss of enthusiasm. Dempsey, more than two decades later, is still one of the best known and revered personalities in the world of sports. How magnificently solunar returns work out!

Farewell to a Friend

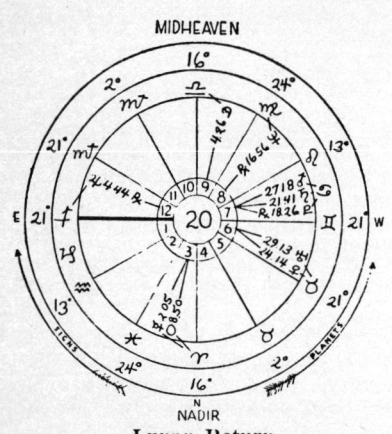

Lunar Return
of Elizabeth Aldrich
Preceding Demise
April 23, 1948
0:25 A. M., L.M.T.,
New York City

Elizabeth Aldrich, known and loved throughout the whole astrological fraternity, both here and abroad, took leave of us on April 28th, 1948, and we are all the better for her having passed our way, to join us—or cause us to join. The Astrologer's Guild of America is particularly in loving indebtedness to her for she had been one of its founders and faithful champions. Many of her friends will reminisce that her hand at making delicious eggnogs and writing poetry was matched only by her skill as a practical astrologer. She did so much for astrology in many ways and was so admired everywhere in her profession, your writer likes to think that her death marked the close of an Elizabethan era on the local scene. She was born at 11:55 a. m., L.M.T., May 17th, 1875, in Des Moines, Iowa.

We include her fatal lunar return here as we feel that it is a superb example of the typical chart to be found as the precursor of natural demise. The three benefics, Venus, Jupiter and Uranus, are in the background, as are the opposed Moon and Sun, with Mercury. The only foreground planets are the malefics, Mars and Saturn, conjunct Pluto in the 7th house. Neptune occupies the 8th house. Complete dissipation of the vital reserve, resulting in surrender of the breath of life, was written everywhere throughout the chart. Passing came as a relief from suffering, shown by the aspects to Jupiter. That our gallant lady had reached some sort of crossroads in her existence during the sidereal month charted was plain from the fact that a background Full Moon was the major configuration.

How suitable to this circumstance was a beautiful poem Elizabeth once penned about death, entitled, "The Pilgrim," which was a voicing of her belief in a Hereafter, comparing death to a journey. The 9th-house Moon is opposed to Mercury and Sol in the 3rd, apt indication that Elizabeth herself was ready to travel that pilgrimage path that leads far, far beyond our mediocre, mortal ken.

Those Fell Clutches

To be arrested, at some time or other during one's life, happens to about one out of every eighteen Americans, according to a recent statistical report which startled us as jarringly as did the fact that one out of every ten first-born Americans is technically illegitimate. Recognition of the real state of affairs in modern civilization bids us give up that air of Puritanical prudery which has long been fashionable in writing for publication. (Decades ago, Robert L. Stevensen complained that there were some things an English author dare not say; fortunately, times have changed enough that frank writers are not now denied a decent burial.) The astrologer, as necessarily as any other professional counsellor, should be awake to reality and think objectively, for only by being realistic can he or she be of genuinely worthwhile service to humankind. It is this personal policy of calling a spade a spade that allows us freedom from hesitation to present examples of astrological merit which might not come under the (hypocritical) heading of conventionality.

One such instance is the case of a man who was arrested on a morals charge for knowingly cavorting with a girl considerably "under age," according to the letter of the (local) law. He was no obscene "monster" or dandy, but simply a typical American male whose path had intersected that of a particularly œstrous, pretty little imp, whose charms would trouble even Cromwell, or the Sinaitic law-giver himself, no less. Had this man known his astrological indications for the

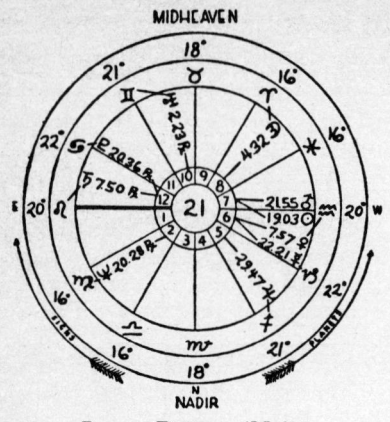

**Lunar Return (Male)
Preceding Arrest**

period and place in which he was trundled off to jail, he might never have been caught in **flagrante delicto** or otherwise. Or maybe the Bard of Avon, himself a shot-gun marriage victim, was right, after all, in saying, ".... hanging and wiving go by destiny."

These indications had been crystalline clear: The Sun conjunct Mars on the 7th cusp could augur little else besides an encounter with the pinions of the law for an act-of-self of a 7th-house nature. Had he, through knowledge of this danger, averted the incident, perhaps the worst that might have happened during that period is a brawl with another fellow. But, as it happened, our paramour was tapped masterfully and told to come along quietly, by a pair of burly vice officers in crepe-sole shoes. He remembers that night in jail as by far the coldest night he ever spent. All that came of the incident was the forfeiture of bail, which in some cases is always set as high as the fine would be if the defendant chose to appear in court. To be sure, after that experience, he never again saw the imp, and will henceforth be more discreet in his selection of playmates, unless he hies himself off to another state where the age-limits, or else the wages of sin, are lower.

The Moon is in the 8th house where it trines Saturn, bespeaking the loss of the bail money, which, incidentally, he had to borrow from a friend (Moon sextile Venus). That he had to pay for his pleasures is surely the action of the nearly-partile opposition of Venus and Saturn from the 6th to the 12th house (confinement). The other opposition in the chart which aided the shaping up of the whole regrettable situation is that between Mercury and Pluto, also involving the 6th and 12th houses, for this invariably implies running counter to law. Aside from that critical Sun-Mars conjunction, the only other angular planet is Uranus in the 10th house. The delights which brought about this whole mess were obviously to the fore, to be taken for the asking (Venus trine, and Moon sextile, Uranus).

He Let George Do It

The annals of crime are continually being written, but every now and then, sporadically through the years, a case turns up which shocks a whole nation and finds the cups of newspaper publishers running over. Such a journalistic Golden Egg was the arrest and trial, for three murders and a hundred thefts, of a 17-year old University of Chicago student in 1946. He was the killer, you may remember, who painted a plea, on the wall of a victim's apartment with her own lipstick, which read, "For heaven's sake catch me before I kill more! I cannot help myself." William Heirens was his name. He was born at 8:40 p. m., L.M.T., on November 15th, 1928, in Chicago, Illinois, a city as famous for its bizarre crimes as London is for English accents.

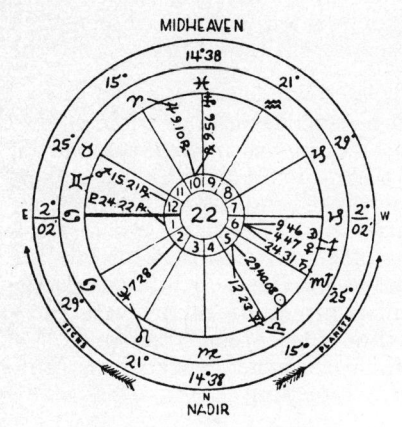

Nativity of Wm. Heirens
(Alias George Murmans)
Born November 15, 1928
8:51 P. M., L.M.T.,
Chicago, Illinois

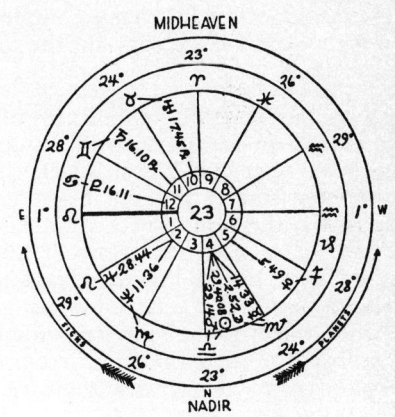

Heirens' Solar Return
Preceding First Murder
November 15, 1944
11:17 P. M., L.M.T.,
Chicago, Illinois

What is most fantastic about this youth Heirens is that he was one of those few bonafide instances of a "double personality," a genuine Dr. Jekyll-Mr. Hyde, as ever was. He, as Willy H., was not the culprit; why, Willy wouldn't hurt a fly. It was George, George Murmans, who was the killer and the robber. Willy had a splendid scholastic record, went to Church and confession faithfully (his mother was a redoubtable religious woman, a very able mother and housekeeper), and was well liked by everybody, it seemed. But once in a while, the consciousness of William Heirens would undergo a black-out. In its place reared up the fearsome George Murmans who used William's body to roam Chicago's dark allies and up fire-escapes in search of prey or loot. George, when apprehended by the police in the act of burglary, admitted the killings, confessing that he experienced sexual satisfaction in the deeds.

The case of Heirens-Murmans has made psychiatric as well as police history. Among the uncanny results of his psychoanalysis was the discovery that he was almost totally anæsthesic, or insensitive to pain. Needles stuck far beneath his fingernails and into the skin of his face and elsewhere induced no reaction, as he did not feel them; what wincing he did was when the test was severe. A closed safety pin tapped against his eyeball did not make him wink or flinch in any way. How interesting this is when we note that the ancient Roman astrologer-poet Manilius said of the constellation Cancer: "Their bodies shall be strong, **inured to pain,** their wits contriving, and intent on gain." The constellation Cancer is on the Ascendant of Heirens' birthchart, with Pluto near the horizon. His nativity is here shown for the record (it has been completely delineated in the author's work on criminogenic factors in the horoscope, entitled "Crime and the Horoscope").

Strangely enough, his progressed horoscope fails to yield highly correlative indications, even though such things as intentional murder and larceny are plainly to be classed as acts-of-self and the projections of inborn (natal) tendencies. Perhaps those who support the theory of astral obsession have a solid case, after all. We are most interested in seeing what at least one of the two solar returns under which he mercilessly killed innocent people shows in the way of correlative indications of the act. The lunar returns attending each of the three murders are astonishingly violent. For our present purpose, we demonstrate with the solar return which preceded Heirens', or Murman's if you wish, first adventure in death-dealing.

The ancient astrologers contended, and even today we concur with them, that a conjunction of the Sun and Moon is malevolent. Heirens' solar return found such a conjunction in the foreground, in further conjunction with destructive, sadistical Mars. As he cried in desperation, "I cannot help myself!" we marvel at the compulsive power of such a configuration to completely overwhelm and control a personality. The psychiatric investigation revealed, interestingly, that he killed only females because they represented, to his tormented subconscious mind, projections of his mother's hated image. Heirens was probably never aware of the psychological motives prompting him to bloodlust, even though he had studied a smattering of depth psychology. How clearly this tragic frame of mind is shown in this, the chart of his initial killing:The Sun, Moon and Mars, all huddled together in the 4th house, signifying the self (Sun) seeking revenge (Mars) on his mother (Moon, 4th). Uranus is in the 10th, where it implies an uppermost urge to do something drastic, unique, and, to him, thrilling (psychiatrists learned that the deed was committed in a state of tumescence).

The keynote of the chart would escape attention if comparison with the natal theme were not made. That is the transit of Saturn over Heirens' radix Mars, placed here in the 11th-house of fulfilled hopes. (His other two murders took place when both transitting Mars and Saturn were on his radix Ascendant.) There is no more terrible, destructive combination than Mars-Saturn. In addition to this unleashing of unbridled Martian impulse into Heirens' life, as shown by this solar return, we have such typical signs of distaste for law as the trine of angular Mercury to 12th-house Pluto, and the transit of Neptune square radix Moon, conjunction radix I. C., and opposition radix Uranus. Mars-Saturn criminality would by itself be more out in the open, but the dark, sinister prominence of Neptune (newsmen called Heirens, "the Cobra") allowed the fiend to pursue his nefarious ends with remarkable cunning and secretiveness. From this and other studies, we are convinced that solunar returns, as analytic tools, are far superior to any other astrological technique yet offered. Had we banked solely on the progressed horoscope, we would have been at a loss to account for the deeds of this creature, unique among the sons of men, who lived among us as a fine fellow during the day and stalked the streets as a werewolf at night.

Go Right to the Source for Your Information

Was Tom Mooney really guilty of the crime he was charged with? Did King Edward merely use his affection for Wally Simpson to escape royal responsibilities, or was he truly so in love an empire could not stand in the way of its consummation? Was Trotsky's assassin an erstwhile friend momentarily maddened, or was Jacson an agent sent by Trotsky's enemies to accomplish the deed? Given acceptable birth data, the astrologer should be able to render a fairly reliable judgment in answer to such questions, or there is nothing to astrology. The Duke's, Mooney's and Trotsky's birthdata are available, so the solution of such perrenial riddles should pose few hindrances to the capable student of astrology. Subjecting these example cases to solunar investigation, we are afforded strikingly plain results, simply arrived at. (Contrast the complexity of most modern astrological methods with the simplicity of solunar interpretation.)

Mooney's Moon

At 2:06 p. m., P.S.T., on July 12th, 1916, a bomb concealed in a satchel exploded at the corner of Stuart and Market in San Francisco, interrupting a "Preparedness Day" parade. Ten persons were killed and forty were injured. Authorities quickly arrested iron moulder and labor organizer Thomas J. Mooney, along with his wife and three other union men, and slapped murder charges on the lot of them. Mrs. Mooney and one of the men were acquitted, while another man was released without a trial. Mooney's companion, Warren K. Billings, was sentenced to life imprisonment, but Mooney received the death penalty. However, thanks to the intercession of President Wilson on

November 28th, 1918, Mooney's sentence was commuted to life-imprisonment. For two decades thereafter, efforts by his friends, sympathizers, and the liberal movement generally, were made to free him, in the firm belief that he had been convicted on perjured testimony. Finally, in fulfillment of a campaign promise, newly-elected Governor Olson of California pardoned Mooney unconditionally on January 7th, 1939. Aged and maligned, Tom Mooney walked out of San Quentin into free air and the arms of his faithful wife.

The Mooney saga is one of America's most controversial historic episodes. The whole drama hinged on the great question, whether or not Tom Mooney actually perpetrated the bombing, or was in any way guilty of participation or conspiracy toward that end. His lunar return preceding the incident is highly revealing. Mars is at the Midheaven, and the Sun and Saturn are conjoined in the 8th house, and at the Midheaven of his locality chart. The Moon and Uranus are squared in the background, Mars is on his radix Uranus, among several other indices of a daring or criminogenic leaning. Even a novice can see immediately that we have here the chart of a man who risked much to cause a commotion, and was **not** railroaded unfairly into prison. It's just not nice to bomb parades, especially if the mayor is marching in it, and, while the bomber probably did not want anybody hurt, lover of the little people that he was, tragedy struck dozens of commoner's homes because of his heartfelt "protest" against national military preparedness.

The lunar return for his final release is a dilly, clearly describing the eventuality, and in a very amusing way, at that. The Moon and Venus are conjoined at the 12th cusp, to the exact minute of arc: After 22 years in stir, we can only try to imagine the man's feelings as he again breathed free air, basked in the glow of a wife's pent-up affection, and realized that he had thousands of friends he had never even known. Notice, in the light of an official dictum in his favor, that Mercury is on the Ascendant, conjunct radix Sun, and that the Sun and Jupiter are sextile. Study also the major transits to natal planets, as they yield much that is enlightening to the discerning student.

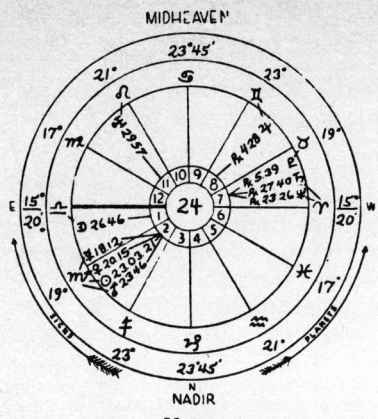

Natus
Thomas J. Mooney
Born December 8, 1882
4:09 A. M., L.M.T.,
Chicago, Illinois

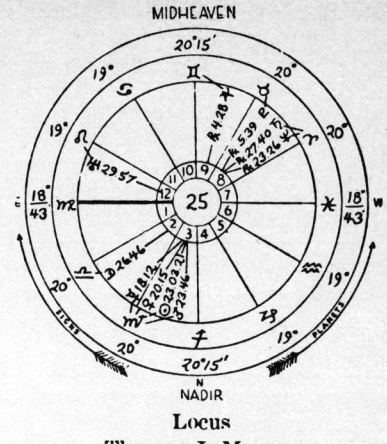

Locus
Thomas J. Mooney
Birthchart Equated
To San Francisco, California

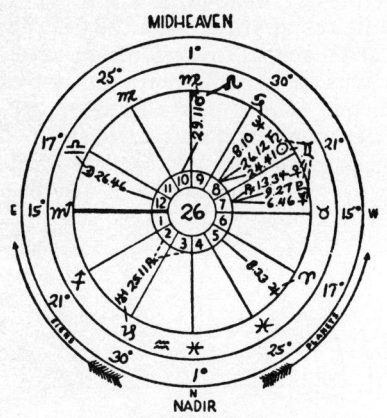

Lunar Return
Preceding Parade Bombing
July 10, 1916
4:28 P. M., L.M.T.,
San Francisco, California

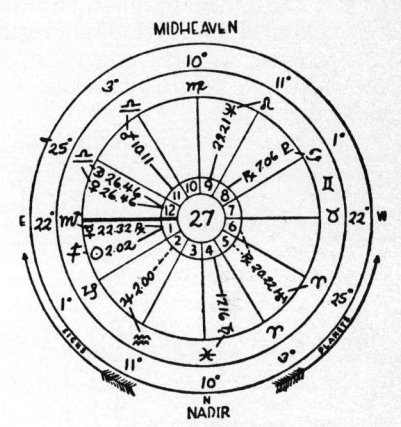

Lunar Return
Preceding Full Pardon
December 18, 1938
6:29 A. M., L.M.T.,
San Quentin, California

A Royal Flush

That Edward did not particularly like being King is evident, first of all, from his birthchart, which shows the Moon rising in Aquarius. Persons with the Moon in the constellation Aquarius tend to shun the limelight, for statistics show that position rating lowest in the charts of politicians. (1200 congressmen and state governors, both incumbent and ex-ed, were studied.) Furthermore, Edward's Sun is in Gemini, so the endless sophistication and limitations forced upon the royally-born were a constant source of boredom to his variety- and freedom-loving soul. The former King cannot be accused of any form of political malingering, when he gave up the crown, for there can be no doubt but that he was truly and enthrallingly in love with Wally.

One sweep of the eye over the present Duke of Windsor's solar and lunar returns preceding his abdication (decision handed the Prime Minister at 8:48 p. m., G.M.T., December 9th, 1936), tells without hedging that his motive was purely a romantic one. Note the triple conjunction of the Sun, Venus and Mars in his annual chart, and the rising of Jupiter and Venus (square Mars) in the monthly figure. These are tokens of falling helplessly in love, if anything is. There are also indications of retirement, resignation, and the conflict of conscience, in both charts, so Edward's sensational decision to let somebody else keep the throne warm was in keeping with his astrological destiny. Love had triumphed, and who but stuffy dowagers would dare deny Dan Cupid a day in his own court?

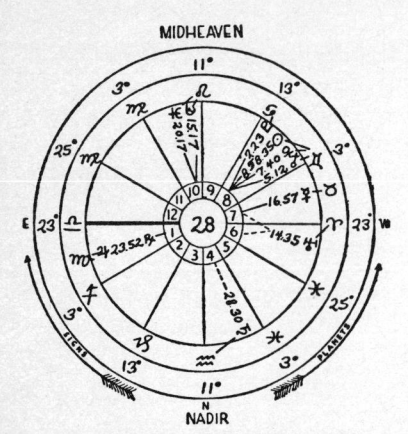

Edward's Solar Return
Preceding Abdication
June 24, 1936
4:17 P. M., G.M.T.,
London, England

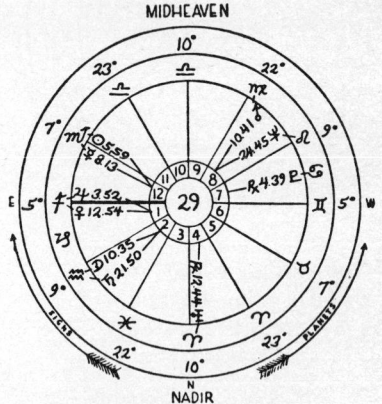

Edward's Lunar Return
Preceding Abdication
November 22, 1936
10:10 A. M., G.M.T.,
London, England

More Than Mayhem in Mexico

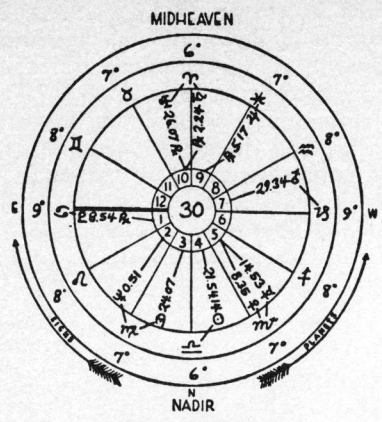

Leon Trotsky
Last Solar Return
November 8, 1939
10:42 P. M., L.M.T.,
Coyoacan, Mexico City

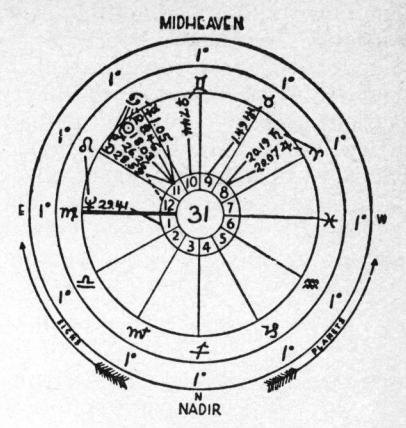

Leon Trotsky
Last Lunar Return
August 4, 1940
8:46 A. M., L.M.T.,
Coyoacan, Mexico City

Leon Trotsky was a man of mystery to the world, but even more so, he was a teller of tall tales. Born with Cancer and the Moon rising, partile square Mars, Trotsky was himself a dramatization of the image-creating, shadow-boxing horoscope he was born with.* Forced to resign, and later exiled by a government he claimed mercilessly blood-purged every insubordinate, Trotsky became the leader of a world-wide revolutionary movement. His last years were spent in a well-fortified villa on the outskirts of Mexico City (paid for by?), in which he headquartered a vast propaganda mill, and wrote several weighty tomes about subjects on which he could not possibly have been an authority.

It is astonishing how many versions of the story of his murder are popularly circulated, even though the assassin's full confession is a matter of public record. Frank Jacson, possessor of many unintelligible aliases, openly admitted that his sole reason for using that Alpine pick-axe on Leon's head was resentment for not being allowed to marry one Sylvia Ageloff. The assault took place on August 20th, 1940, but Trotsky managed to keep body and soul together until the day following. Trotskyites the world over have been claiming that their leader's death was perpetrated by subversives (!) who had infiltrated into their ranks purposely to silence the proletarian messiah.

Jacson's confession is more likely nearer the truth than any of the legends current nowadays, according to the testimony of the solar

* Leon Trotsky was born at Yanovka, 2½ miles from Gromokley, near Odessa, in the Ukraine, at 10:09 p. m., L.M.T., November 7th, 1879.

and lunar returns prior to Trotsky's silencing. It was the year of his downfall, for one thing, for Saturn is at the Midheaven, with afflicted Sun in the 4th, telling what kind of downfall was in store. Pluto rising, and Sun opposed to Uranus, hints of the man's irascible and stubborn nature, as he became more and more intensified in forwarding his own "cause," demanding ridiculous personal sacrifices of his workers. Mars in the 7th house, afflicting the Sun-Uranus alignment, was a harbinger of disastrous consequences for irritating a partner or co-worker. Note that the immediate source of the clash was a 7th-house subject (marital and co-operative affairs). Most telling is the close T-square completed by foreground Mars with the natal square of Moon and Mars.

More detail is shown in the lunar return, where we find a stellium of astonishing malevolence in the 11th house, which rules, primarily, one's relationship to his "friends," organizations and "causes." The Moon is in close conjunction with Mars, while the Sun is closely squared by conjoined Saturn and Jupiter in the 8th and Aries (the "head"). Neptune is rising, indicating treachery and victimization. So, a friend, not a secret enemy, bludgeoned Trotsky's cranium, for a secret enemy would have entailed a 6th-house factor. The confession of the murderer, then, may be accepted at its face value; there is nothing in these charts to warrant the belief that some great international conspiracy was at the bottom of the homicide.

CHAPTER 7

CRISES IN CONSCIOUSNESS

TRANSITS to both natal and progressed planets bring about the kaleidoscopic variety of experiences in life. Now and then, there is a concentration of close transits to critical points in the natus, which results in some kind of **crisis in experience**, appropriate to the compounded natures of the planets involved in the concentration. It is these climaxes in the "stream of consciousness" which upset the philosophical apple-cart when it comes to the riddle of Free Will.

It goes without saying, and it is so obviously true that to quibble with dissenters is a waste of time, that transits to natal planets are more nearly partile in the sidereal zodiac, at the times of important events in the life, than when measured in the tropical zodiac. This is because the tropical zodiac does not account for the precessional effect which amounts to a full degree in about 72 years. Hence, the older one gets, the larger becomes the amount of precession, and as the years slip by, appropriate events **apparently** tend to occur later and later after the partile phase of the transit has passed. No such discrepancy is evident in working directly with an SZ ephemeris, for the precessional effect is automatically taken care of.

According to his confession, "The Fox," William Edward Hickman,* murdered little Marian Parker at 7:30 a. m., P.S.T., on December 17th, 1927, in Los Angeles. Since to deliberately commit a mutilation murder is almost completely an act-of-self, we would expect his progressed chart to be more pregnant than transits with indices of violent compulsions. It does, and to such an astounding degree that the writer respects this case as a classic among the momentous horoscopes in his collection.

Progressed Moon	21°02′	Virgo
Radical Mars	21 21	Pisces
Radical Neptune	19 12	Gemini
Progressed Neptune	18 47	Gemini
Radical Uranus	20 54	Sagittarius
Progressed Uranus	21 53	Sagittarius

Hickman's criminogenic urges could well have spent their fury within a week or two before or after the actual time of the murder. Therefore, there must have been a transit-caused **crisis in consciousness** to have "timed" the tragic hour. Note how the transitting Sun and Moon touched off vital points in his horoscope, by considering the following tally:

---

* Wm. Edw. Hickman was born at 3:57 a. m., L.M.T., on January 31st, 1909, at 35° North and 94½° West. His mother had been in labor for 36 hours, and his father thought it was a stillbirth, since the babe was "black."

—— 83 ——

Trans. Sun	square	rad. Saturn	by 0°05',	applying
Trans. Moon	conjunct	rad. Neptune	by 0 17,	separating
Trans. Moon	conjunct	prog. Neptune	by 0 08,	applying
Trans. Jupiter	conjunct	rad. Saturn	by 0 09,	separating
Trans. Neptune	trine	rad. Mars	by 0 10,	separating.

With the victim a captive at his mercy for 43¼ hours, it was not until the transiting planets created a concentration of adverse pressures that a crisis in Hickman's consciousness released the ghoulish urges shown at a peak in his progressions.

Another excellent demonstration of the lucidity with which transits foment a crisis in the experience of a soul is the case of William Heirens at the time of his accidental apprehension by the police. (His birthchart is given in the sixth chapter.) Caught prowling on a fire escape by a wary apartment-dweller who telephoned the police, Heirens was knocked unconscious by a deftly-tossed flower pot, at midnight of June 25th-26th, 1946, in Chicago. Taken to jail and booked on suspicion of burglary, it was several weeks before police discovered that the 17-year old was the mass murderer they were seeking. His transits, at the time his pot-luck was so poor, were these:

Trans. Sun	square	rad. Uranus	by 0°00',	partile
Trans. Sun	opposition	rad. Moon	by 0 10,	separating
Trans. Moon	opposition	rad. Sun	by 0 37,	applying
Trans. Jupiter	square	rad. Pluto	by 0 48,	applying
Trans. Mars	trine	rad. Jupiter	by 0 07,	separating
Trans. Saturn	conjunct	rad. Ascendant	by 0 54,	applying
Trans. Uranus	opposition	rad. Saturn	by 0 02,	applying

Already pointed out earlier in this book, as an astrological pitfall, was the fact that major aspects may be found at work at any random moment. The student who feels anxiety over an approaching "bad aspect" actually has little license for his fear, if there is no simultaneous bundling of other transits. To be sure, **all** astrological influences are responded to in one way or another; it is safe to say, nevertheless, that at least 95% of all transitive forces induce only psychological reactions. In other words, the oscillation of your moods, from day to day and from hour to hour, is traceable to transitive influences. Once in a while, a series of transits is synchronized, as in the two examples just cited, when it is advisable to withdraw yourself from any scene or situation in which there is the slimmest suggestion of potential trouble.

These "crises" in experience may be anticipated by the efficient student of astrology. Moreover, there are as many, if not more, of these crises when the actual fulfillment is a fortunate event. Hence, to apply astrology in order to derive heaven-sent benefits, take advantage of these favorable concentrations of transits, to further your social, romantic, and business interests. Don't fret over an impending transit of Saturn, say, for the odds have it that you will merely feel weary, forget a few names and faces, and become overly resentful of having to "clean up after" other people. If Mars is the offender, restrain the impulse to throw something at him if the neighbor's dog digs up your pansy patch. A person whose system floods with adrenalin in anticipation of imagined terrors lurking ahead is psychologically unfit to study astrology. A student afraid of malefic indications has not grounded himself well in the magnificent philosophy of astrology to begin with, nor has he had enough practical experience with observational astrology to enable him to evaluate clearly.

Don't Belittle Locality Charts!

As with most controversial topics in any field of study, there is often more argumentation from both sides than straightforward efforts to settle the question through evidence based upon research. The time that is wasted upon debate could better be devoted to proving or disproving the salient proposition. One of these controversies in the astrological field has to do with the validity of what is known as "locality-chart equation." We have noted with dismay that the primary argument used by some against locality-astrology is a hazily quoted passage of Old Testament scripture, inspection of which proves its comical irrelevancy.

The other stock argument, made confidently by the new modernistic school of astrologers, is that the nativity alone suffices to portray the whole pattern of personality and the whole circumference of individual experience. Of course, we agree wholeheartedly with that view, but do not limit the scope of the word "nativity." The birth-chart is a chart of the universe whose center is **the individual**. He remains the center of the universe—or, more correctly, **his** universe—so long as he is incarnate in this world. Wherever he goes over the surface of the earth, he still retains his centricity in the scheme of things.

The results of **observational study** plainly indicate the fact that, so far as eventualities of importance in the life are concerned, the so-called locality chart is as potent, if not more so in several respects, than the familiar radix. To deny this is to deny a mountain of affirmative evidence.

The new student of astrology will naturally want to settle this, and similar issues, to his own satisfaction through private study. However, it will be well to give data for two or three instances which will stimulate general interest in the matter. Two case-histories already touched upon in the present volume offer an interesting opener. Both William Heirens and Edward Hickman committed mutilation murders of young girls, but Heirens killed Suzanne Degnan in Chicago, his own place of birth, while Hickman killed Marian Parker in Los Angeles, more than a thousand miles away from his own birth place. Compare the transitive positions of Mars and Saturn in the two killers' charts, one intact, as of birth, and the other properly equated to the locality at which the deed was committed:

William Heirens' Murder of Little Suzanne Degnan		Edward Hickman's Murder of Little Marian Parker	
Natus Ascendant:	2°02′ Cancer	Locus Ascendant:	9°00′ Scorpio
Trans. Mars:	1 32 Cancer	Trans. Mars:	12 42 Scorpio
Trans. Saturn:	27 41 Gemini	Trans. Saturn:	18 03 Scorpio

Surely, the presence of the two most vicious malefics near the Ascendants of these charts at the time their natives perpetrated diabolic crimes of identical nature can hardly be classed as an amusing coincidence by those who belittle locality-astrology. The Cobra and the Fox had the same overt motive (kidnap for ransom), and both embellished their ghastly work with deliberate dismemberment of their victims.

Even more striking is the birthchart of Winnie Ruth Judd equated to Phoenix, Arizona, the locale of one of America's most shocking double-murders. Winnie Ruth Judd, on the morning of October 17th, 1931, murdered her allegedly two best girl friends, stuffed their bodies into trunks and had these gruesome containers shipped to Los Angeles, where she was apprehended two weeks later. The dramatic crime is so well known it would be repetitious to go into details here now, for our interest lies in the transits to Winnie's locality chart for the time of the horrors.

According to her pastor-father's own biography of Winnie, the murderess-to-be was born at midnight of January 29th-30th, 1905, in the little town of Oxford, Indiana. Her unrectified Natus, then, has a sidereal time of 8:46:09. The same moment of time at Phoenix occurred when the sidereal time was 7:07:05, for the Arizona city is 1:39:04 west of Oxford, Indiana. The wary student will certainly appreciate the significance of the following chart elements, which include the cusps of both Mrs. Judd's radical and locality charts, together with the radix and transiting planetary positions, the latter for the hour of the maniacal killings:

	Natus Houses	Locus Houses
Midheaven	15° ♋ 35′	21° ♊ 56′
11th House	13 ♌	21 ♋
12th House	10 ♍	20 ♌
Ascendant	9 ♎ 22	20 ♍ 40
2nd House	12 ♏	21 ♎
3rd House	15 ♐	21 ♏

	Radix Planets	Transiting Planets
Sun	16° ♑ 11′	29° ♍ 26
Moon	14 ♏ 40	20 ♐ 48
Mercury	22 ♐ 46	28 ♍ 43
Venus	2 ♓ 12	9 ♎ 53
Mars	14 ♎ 24	26 ♎ 58
Jupiter	0 ♈ 05	24 ♋ 35
Saturn	28 ♑ 19	23 ♐ 19
Uranus	8 ♐ 49	23 ♓ 16 ℞
Neptune	12 ♊ 24	13 ♌ 18
Pluto	26 ♉ 19 ℞	28 ♊ 15

The court decided that Winnie was unquestionably insane at the time. Her deterioration on the witness stand alone would have justified that merciful decision. Astrology, in an equally dramatic way, corroborates the fact that Winnie was not in her right mind on that fatal morning, for only a well-integrated person could have survived the planetary pressures on her locality-angles and Mercury without at least a minor shake-up of the consciousness. Winnie was predisposed to dissociation from birth, and the Mercury-Saturn-Uranus influences she was bucking at the time were too great a strain.

Wherever Winnie might have been in the world, she would have suffered the effects of the transiting Saturn-Uranus attack on her natal Mercury. But in moving to Phoenix, she automatically brought her natal Mercury to the Nadir. Saturn astride the mental planet at the "foundation" of her locality chart jarred her very consciousness to its core. The Moon that morning touched off the same angle by conjunction; so much morbid "weight" caused her mentality to "cave in."

Those prone to deny the importance of the locality chart should consider the transits to Winnie's birth place chart. Mind you, when the native murdered her two best friends, transiting Venus was exactly conjunct her Natus Ascendant! Furthermore, Jupiter was within orb of conjunction her radical Midheaven. By no stretch of the imagination can any astrologer worthy of the name find appropriate transitive indices of the event in her horoscope of birth, while the angular transits alone would seem to have blessed the native with a delightfully pleasant morning.

The late Alexander Woolcott's chart is a familiar one in the collections of modern astrological students. Mr. Woolcott, "the man who came to dinner," was born at 3:30 P. M., in Phalanx, New Jersey, on January 19th, 1887. As an illuminating exercise, we suggest that the student equate his chart to San Francisco, California, where, on April 23rd, 1940, he suffered a heart attack which stopped the show in which he was guesting. The City by the Golden Gate, according to locality astrology, was a danger-spot for this talented man. Study his locality chart, and learn why, for it demonstrates to the hilt the importance of the Locus in the precipitation of adverse eventualities.

Those who have the birth data of Bruno Hauptmann, convicted kidnapper of the ill-starred Lindbergh baby, have a case at hand which will once and for all give the lie to the arguments against the value of locality astrology. The historic case of Tom Mooney, in connection with the bombing incident in San Francisco, is another meaty obstacle to locality-astrology opponents. Study cases where the native encountered serious mishaps in places far from his native haunts. You will see that the misfortunes are described most lucidly in the Locus, vaguely, or not at all, in the Natus.

SIDEREAL LONGITUDE OF THE VERNAL POINT

Referred to Spica as Fiducial

Date	Common Years 1849	1850	1851	Leap Year 1852	
	° ′	° ′ ″	° ′ ″		° ′ ″
Jan. 1	♓ 16 01	♓ 15 16	♓ 14 30	Jan. 1	♓ 13 42
Jan. 11	7 15 56	7 15 11	7 14 25	Jan. 11	7 13 37
Jan. 21	7 15 51	7 15 06	7 14 20	Jan. 21	7 13 32
Jan. 31	7 15 46	7 15 01	7 14 15	Jan. 31	7 13 27
Feb. 10	7 15 41	7 14 56	7 14 10	Feb. 10	7 13 22
Feb. 20	7 15 37	7 14 52	7 14 06	Feb. 20	7 13 18
Mar. 2	7 15 33	7 14 49	7 14 02	Mar. 1	7 13 15
Mar. 12	7 15 30	7 14 46	7 13 59	Mar. 11	7 13 12
Mar. 22	7 15 28	7 14 43	7 13 57	Mar. 21	7 13 09
Apr. 1	7 15 26	7 14 41	7 13 55	Mar. 31	7 13 07
Apr. 11	7 15 25	7 14 40	7 13 54	Apr. 10	7 13 06
Apr. 21	7 15 24	7 14 39	7 13 53	Apr. 20	7 13 05
May 1	7 15 24	7 14 39	7 13 52	Apr. 30	7 13 04
May 11	7 15 24	7 14 39	7 13 52	May 10	7 13 04
May 21	7 15 25	7 14 39	7 13 53	May 20	7 13 04
May 31	7 15 25	7 14 40	7 13 53	May 30	7 13 05
June 10	7 15 26	7 14 41	7 13 54	June 9	7 13 06
June 20	7 15 28	7 14 43	7 13 56	June 19	7 13 07
June 30	7 15 29	7 14 44	7 13 57	June 29	7 13 09
July 10	7 15 31	7 14 46	7 13 59	July 9	7 13 10
July 20	7 15 33	7 14 48	7 14 01	July 19	7 13 12
July 30	7 15 35	7 14 50	7 14 03	July 29	7 13 14
Aug. 9	7 15 37	7 14 51	7 14 04	Aug. 8	7 13 16
Aug. 19	7 15 39	7 14 53	7 14 06	Aug. 18	7 13 17
Aug. 29	7 15 41	7 14 55	7 14 08	Aug. 28	7 13 19
Sept. 8	7 15 42	7 14 56	7 14 09	Sept. 7	7 13 20
Sept. 18	7 15 43	7 14 57	7 14 10	Sept. 17	7 13 21
Sept. 28	7 15 44	7 14 58	7 14 11	Sept. 27	7 13 22
Oct. 8	7 15 43	7 14 58	7 14 11	Oct. 7	7 13 22
Oct. 18	7 15 43	7 14 57	7 14 10	Oct. 17	7 13 21
Oct. 28	7 15 41	7 14 56	7 14 08	Oct. 27	7 13 19
Nov. 7	7 15 39	7 14 53	7 14 06	Nov. 6	7 13 17
Nov. 17	7 15 36	7 14 50	7 14 03	Nov. 16	7 13 14
Nov. 27	7 15 33	7 14 47	7 14 00	Nov. 26	7 13 10
Dec. 7	7 15 28	7 14 43	7 13 55	Dec. 6	7 13 06
Dec. 17	7 15 24	7 14 38	7 13 50	Dec. 16	7 13 01
Dec. 27	7 15 19	7 14 33	7 13 45	Dec. 26	7 12 56
Jan. 6	7 15 14	7 14 28	7 13 40	Jan. 5	7 12 51

The sidereal longitude of the vernal point recorded in this standardized Spica Fiducial has been found to differ by approximately 0°06′05″ from the most recent calculations of the Synetic Vernal Point based on values established by observation. This difference should be taken into consideration in the use of these tables.

SIDEREAL LONGITUDE OF THE VERNAL POINT

Referred to Spica as Fiducial

Date		Common Years 1853	1854	1855	Leap Year 1856	
		° ′ ″	° ′ ″	° ′ ″		° ′ ″
Jan.	1	♓ 12 53	♓ 12 01	♓ 11 08	Jan. 1	♓ 10 14
Jan.	11	7 12 47	7 11 56	7 11 03	Jan. 11	7 10 09
Jan.	21	7 12 42	7 11 51	7 10 58	Jan. 21	7 10 03
Jan.	31	7 12 37	7 11 46	7 10 53	Jan. 31	7 09 58
Feb.	10	7 12 32	7 11 41	7 10 48	Feb. 10	7 09 53
Feb.	20	7 12 28	7 11 37	7 10 43	Feb. 20	7 09 49
Mar.	2	7 12 24	7 11 33	7 10 39	Mar. 1	7 09 45
Mar.	12	7 12 21	7 11 30	7 10 36	Mar. 11	7 09 42
Mar.	22	7 12 19	7 11 27	7 10 33	Mar. 21	7 09 39
Apr.	1	7 12 17	7 11 25	7 10 31	Mar. 31	7 09 37
Apr.	11	7 12 15	7 11 24	7 10 30	Apr. 10	7 09 35
Apr.	21	7 12 15	7 11 23	7 10 29	Apr. 20	7 09 34
May	1	7 12 14	7 11 22	7 10 28	Apr. 30	7 09 33
May	11	7 12 14	7 11 22	7 10 28	May 10	7 09 33
May	21	7 12 14	7 11 22	7 10 28	May 20	7 09 33
May	31	7 12 15	7 11 23	7 10 29	May 30	7 09 34
June	10	7 12 16	7 11 24	7 10 30	June 9	7 09 35
June	20	7 12 17	7 11 25	7 10 31	June 19	7 09 36
June	30	7 12 18	7 11 26	7 10 32	June 29	7 09 37
July	10	7 12 20	7 11 27	7 10 33	July 9	7 09 38
July	20	7 12 22	7 11 29	7 10 35	July 19	7 09 40
July	30	7 12 23	7 11 31	7 10 37	July 29	7 09 42
Aug.	9	7 12 25	7 11 33	7 10 38	Aug. 8	7 09 43
Aug.	19	7 12 27	7 11 34	7 10 40	Aug. 18	7 09 45
Aug.	29	7 12 28	7 11 36	7 10 41	Aug. 28	7 09 46
Sept.	8	7 12 30	7 11 37	7 10 42	Sept. 7	7 09 47
Sept.	18	7 12 30	7 11 38	7 10 43	Sept. 17	7 09 48
Sept.	28	7 12 31	7 11 38	7 10 44	Sept. 27	7 09 48
Oct.	8	7 12 31	7 11 38	7 10 43	Oct. 7	7 09 48
Oct.	18	7 12 30	7 11 37	7 10 42	Oct. 17	7 09 47
Oct.	28	7 12 28	7 11 35	7 10 41	Oct. 27	7 09 46
Nov.	7	7 12 26	7 11 33	7 10 38	Nov. 6	7 09 43
Nov.	17	7 12 23	7 11 30	7 10 35	Nov. 16	7 09 40
Nov.	27	7 12 19	7 11 26	7 10 31	Nov. 26	7 09 36
Dec.	7	7 12 14	7 11 21	7 10 27	Dec. 6	7 09 32
Dec.	17	7 12 09	7 11 16	7 10 22	Dec. 16	7 09 27
Dec.	27	7 12 04	7 11 11	7 10 17	Dec. 26	7 09 21
Jan.	6	7 11 59	7 11 06	7 10 12	Jan. 5	7 09 16

SIDEREAL LONGITUDE OF THE VERNAL POINT

Referred to Spica as Fiducial

Date	Common Years 1857	1858	1859	Leap Year 1860	
	° ′ ″	° ′ ″	° ′ ″		° ′ ″
Jan. 1	♓ 09 18	♓ 08 22	♓ 07 27	Jan. 1	♓ 06 32
Jan. 11	7 09 13	7 08 17	7 07 21	Jan. 11	7 06 27
Jan. 21	7 09 07	7 08 11	7 07 16	Jan. 21	7 06 21
Jan. 31	7 09 02	7 08 06	7 07 11	Jan. 31	7 06 16
Feb. 10	7 08 57	7 08 01	7 07 06	Feb. 10	7 06 11
Feb. 20	7 08 53	7 07 57	7 07 01	Feb. 20	7 06 07
Mar. 2	7 08 49	7 07 53	7 06 57	Mar. 1	7 06 03
Mar. 12	7 08 46	7 07 50	7 06 54	Mar. 11	7 06 00
Mar. 22	7 08 43	7 07 47	7 06 51	Mar. 21	7 05 57
Apr. 1	7 08 41	7 07 45	7 06 49	Mar. 31	7 05 55
Apr. 11	7 08 39	7 07 43	7 06 48	Apr. 10	7 05 53
Apr. 21	7 08 38	7 07 42	7 06 47	Apr. 20	7 05 52
May 1	7 08 38	7 07 42	7 06 46	Apr. 30	7 05 52
May 11	7 08 37	7 07 41	7 06 46	May 10	7 05 52
May 21	1 08 38	7 07 42	7 06 46	May 20	7 05 52
May 31	7 08 38	7 07 42	7 06 47	May 30	7 05 52
June 10	7 08 39	7 07 43	7 06 47	June 9	7 05 53
June 20	7 08 40	7 07 44	7 06 48	June 19	7 05 54
June 30	7 08 41	7 07 45	7 06 50	June 29	7 05 56
July 10	7 08 43	7 07 47	7 06 51	July 9	7 05 57
July 20	7 08 44	7 07 48	7 06 53	July 19	7 05 59
July 30	7 08 46	7 07 50	7 06 54	July 29	7 06 00
Aug. 9	7 08 47	7 07 51	7 06 56	Aug. 8	7 06 02
Aug. 19	7 08 49	7 07 53	7 06 58	Aug. 18	7 06 04
Aug. 29	7 08 50	7 07 54	7 06 59	Aug. 28	7 06 05
Sept. 8	7 08 52	7 07 56	7 07 00	Sept. 7	7 06 07
Sept. 18	7 08 52	7 07 56	7 07 01	Sept. 17	7 06 07
Sept. 28	7 08 53	7 07 57	7 07 01	Sept. 27	7 06 08
Oct. 8	7 08 53	7 07 56	7 07 01	Oct. 7	7 06 08
Oct. 18	7 08 51	7 07 55	7 07 00	Oct. 17	7 06 07
Oct. 28	7 08 49	7 07 54	7 06 59	Oct. 27	7 06 05
Nov. 7	7 08 47	7 07 51	7 06 56	Nov. 6	7 06 03
Nov. 17	7 08 44	7 07 48	7 06 53	Nov. 16	7 06 00
Nov. 27	7 08 40	7 07 44	7 06 49	Nov. 26	7 05 56
Dec. 7	7 08 35	7 07 40	7 06 45	Dec. 6	7 05 52
Dec. 17	7 08 30	7 07 35	7 06 40	Dec. 16	7 05 47
Dec. 27	7 08 25	7 07 30	7 06 35	Dec. 26	7 05 42
Jan. 6	7 08 20	7 07 25	7 06 30	Jan. 5	7 05 37

SIDEREAL LONGITUDE OF THE VERNAL POINT

Referred to Spica as Fiducial

Date	Common Years 1861	1862	1863	Leap Year 1864	
	° ′ ″	° ′ ″	° ′ ″		° ′ ″
Jan. 1	♓ 05 38	♓ 04 47	♓ 03 58	Jan. 1	♓ 03 10
Jan. 11	7 05 33	7 04 42	7 03 52	Jan. 11	7 03 05
Jan. 21	7 05 27	7 04 36	7 03 47	Jan. 21	7 03 00
Jan. 31	7 05 22	7 04 31	7 03 42	Jan. 31	7 02 55
Feb. 10	7 05 17	7 04 27	7 03 37	Feb. 10	7 02 50
Feb. 20	7 05 13	7 04 22	7 03 33	Feb. 20	7 02 46
Mar. 2	7 05 10	7 04 19	7 03 30	Mar. 1	7 02 42
Mar. 12	7 05 07	7 04 16	7 03 27	Mar. 11	7 02 39
Mar. 22	7 05 04	7 04 13	7 03 24	Mar. 21	7 02 37
Apr. 1	7 05 02	7 04 11	7 03 22	Mar. 31	7 02 35
Apr. 11	7 05 00	7 04 10	7 03 21	Apr. 10	7 02 34
Apr. 21	7 05 00	7 04 09	7 03 20	Apr. 20	7 02 33
May 1	7 04 59	7 04 08	7 03 19	Apr. 30	7 02 32
May 11	7 04 59	7 04 08	7 03 19	May 10	7 02 32
May 21	7 04 59	7 04 09	7 03 20	May 20	7 02 33
May 31	7 05 00	7 04 09	7 03 20	May 30	7 02 33
June 10	7 05 01	7 04 10	7 03 21	June 9	7 02 34
June 20	7 05 02	7 04 11	7 03 23	June 19	7 02 36
June 30	7 05 03	7 04 13	7 03 24	June 29	7 02 37
July 10	7 05 05	7 04 14	7 03 26	July 9	7 02 39
July 20	7 05 07	7 04 16	7 03 28	July 19	7 02 41
July 30	7 05 08	7 04 18	7 03 30	July 29	7 02 43
Aug. 9	7 05 10	7 04 20	7 03 31	Aug. 8	7 02 45
Aug. 19	7 05 12	7 04 22	7 03 33	Aug. 18	7 02 46
Aug. 29	7 05 13	7 04 23	7 03 35	Aug. 28	7 02 48
Sept. 8	7 05 15	7 04 25	7 03 36	Sept. 7	7 02 50
Sept. 18	7 05 15	7 04 26	7 03 37	Sept. 17	7 02 51
Sept. 28	7 05 16	7 04 26	7 03 38	Sept. 27	7 02 51
Oct. 8	7 05 16	7 04 26	7 03 38	Oct. 7	7 02 51
Oct. 18	7 05 15	7 04 25	7 03 37	Oct. 17	7 02 51
Oct. 28	7 05 13	7 04 24	7 03 36	Oct. 27	7 02 49
Nov. 7	7 05 11	7 04 21	7 03 33	Nov. 6	7 02 47
Nov. 17	7 05 08	7 04 18	7 03 30	Nov. 16	7 02 44
Nov. 27	7 05 04	7 04 14	7 03 27	Nov. 26	7 02 41
Dec. 7	7 05 00	7 04 10	7 03 22	Dec. 6	7 02 36
Dec. 17	7 04 55	7 04 05	7 03 18	Dec. 16	7 02 32
Dec. 27	7 04 50	7 04 00	7 03 13	Dec. 26	7 02 27
Jan. 6	7 04 45	7 03 55	7 03 08	Jan. 5	7 02 22

SIDEREAL LONGITUDE OF THE VERNAL POINT

Referred to Spica as Fiducial

Date		Common Years 1865	1866	1867	Leap Year 1868		
		° ′ ″	° ′ ″	° ′ ″			° ′ ″
Jan.	1	♓ 02 24	♓ 01 39	♓ 00 54	Jan.	1	♓ 00 10
Jan.	11	7 02 18	7 01 33	7 00 49	Jan.	11	7 00 05
Jan.	21	7 02 13	7 01 28	7 00 44	Jan.	21	7 00 00
Jan.	31	7 02 08	7 01 23	7 00 39	Jan.	31	6 59 55
Feb.	10	7 02 04	7 01 19	7 00 35	Feb.	10	6 59 50
Feb.	20	7 02 00	7 01 15	7 00 30	Feb.	20	6 59 46
Mar.	2	7 01 56	7 01 11	7 00 27	Mar.	1	6 59 43
Mar.	12	7 01 53	7 01 08	7 00 24	Mar.	11	6 59 40
Mar.	22	7 01 51	7 01 06	7 00 22	Mar.	21	6 59 37
Apr.	1	7 01 49	7 01 04	7 00 20	Mar.	31	6 59 35
Apr.	11	7 01 48	7 01 03	7 00 18	Apr.	10	6 59 34
Apr.	21	7 01 47	7 01 02	7 00 18	Apr.	20	6 59 33
May	1	7 01 47	7 01 02	7 00 17	Apr.	30	6 59 33
May	11	7 01 47	7 01 02	7 00 17	May	10	6 59 33
May	21	7 01 47	7 01 02	7 00 18	May	20	6 59 33
May	31	7 01 48	7 01 03	7 00 19	May	30	6 59 34
June	10	7 01 49	7 01 04	7 00 20	June	9	6 59 35
June	20	7 01 50	7 01 06	7 00 21	June	19	6 59 36
June	30	7 01 52	7 01 07	7 00 23	June	29	6 59 38
July	10	7 01 54	7 01 09	7 00 24	July	9	6 59 40
July	20	7 01 56	7 01 11	7 00 26	July	19	6 59 42
July	30	7 01 57	7 01 13	7 00 28	July	29	6 59 43
Aug.	9	7 01 59	7 01 15	7 00 30	Aug.	8	6 59 45
Aug.	19	7 02 01	7 01 17	7 00 32	Aug.	18	6 59 47
Aug.	29	7 02 03	7 01 18	7 00 34	Aug.	28	6 59 49
Sept.	8	7 02 04	7 01 20	7 00 35	Sept.	7	6 59 50
Sept.	18	7 02 05	7 01 21	7 00 36	Sept.	17	6 59 52
Sept.	28	7 02 06	7 01 21	7 00 37	Sept.	27	6 59 52
Oct.	8	7 02 06	7 01 21	7 00 37	Oct.	7	6 59 52
Oct.	18	7 02 05	7 01 21	7 00 36	Oct.	17	6 59 51
Oct.	28	7 02 04	7 01 19	7 00 35	Oct.	27	6 59 50
Nov.	7	7 02 02	7 01 17	7 00 33	Nov.	6	6 59 48
Nov.	17	7 01 59	7 01 14	7 00 30	Nov.	16	6 59 45
Nov.	27	7 01 56	7 01 11	7 00 26	Nov.	26	6 59 41
Dec.	7	7 01 51	7 01 06	7 00 22	Dec.	6	6 59 37
Dec.	17	7 01 46	7 01 02	7 00 18	Dec.	16	6 59 32
Dec.	27	7 01 41	7 00 57	7 00 13	Dec.	26	6 59 27
Jan.	6	7 01 36	7 00 52	7 00 08	Jan.	5	6 59 22

SIDEREAL LONGITUDE OF THE VERNAL POINT

Referred to Spica as Fiducial

Date		Common Years			Leap Year		
		1869	1870	1871	1872		
		° ′ ″	° ′ ″	° ′ ″			° ′ ″
Jan.	1	♓ 59 24	♓ 58 38	♓ 57 50	Jan.	1	♓ 57 00
Jan.	11	6 59 19	6 58 33	6 57 44	Jan.	11	6 56 54
Jan.	21	6 59 15	6 58 28	6 57 39	Jan.	21	6 56 49
Jan.	31	6 59 09	6 58 23	6 57 34	Jan.	31	6 56 44
Feb.	10	6 59 05	6 58 18	6 57 29	Feb.	10	6 56 39
Feb.	20	6 59 00	6 58 14	6 57 25	Feb.	20	6 56 35
Mar.	2	6 58 57	6 58 10	6 57 22	Mar.	1	6 56 31
Mar.	12	6 58 54	6 58 07	6 57 18	Mar.	11	6 56 28
Mar.	22	6 58 52	6 58 05	6 57 16	Mar.	21	6 56 26
Apr.	1	6 58 50	6 58 03	6 57 14	Mar.	31	6 56 23
Apr.	11	6 58 48	6 58 01	6 57 13	Apr.	10	6 56 22
Apr.	21	6 58 48	6 58 01	6 57 12	Apr.	20	6 56 21
May	1	6 58 47	6 58 00	6 57 11	Apr.	30	6 56 20
May	11	6 58 47	6 58 00	6 57 11	May	10	6 56 20
May	21	6 58 48	6 58 00	6 57 11	May	20	6 56 20
May	31	6 58 48	6 58 01	6 57 12	May	30	6 56 21
June	10	6 58 49	6 58 02	6 57 13	June	9	6 56 22
June	20	6 58 51	6 58 03	6 57 14	June	19	6 56 23
June	30	6 58 52	6 58 05	6 57 15	June	29	6 56 24
July	10	6 58 54	6 58 07	6 57 17	July	9	6 56 26
July	20	6 58 56	6 58 08	6 57 19	July	19	6 56 27
July	30	6 58 58	6 58 10	6 57 21	July	29	6 56 29
Aug.	9	6 59 00	6 58 12	6 57 22	Aug.	8	6 56 31
Aug.	19	6 59 01	6 58 14	6 57 24	Aug.	18	6 56 33
Aug.	29	6 59 03	6 58 15	6 57 26	Aug.	28	6 56 34
Sept.	8	6 59 04	6 58 17	6 57 27	Sept.	7	6 56 35
Sept.	18	6 59 05	6 58 18	6 57 28	Sept.	17	6 56 36
Sept.	28	6 59 06	6 58 19	6 57 28	Sept.	27	6 56 37
Oct.	8	6 59 06	6 58 18	6 57 28	Oct.	7	6 56 36
Oct.	18	6 59 05	6 58 17	6 57 27	Oct.	17	6 56 36
Oct.	28	6 59 04	6 58 16	6 57 26	Oct.	27	6 56 34
Nov.	7	6 59 01	6 58 13	6 57 23	Nov.	6	6 56 32
Nov.	17	6 58 58	6 58 10	6 57 20	Nov.	16	6 56 29
Nov.	27	6 58 54	6 58 06	6 57 17	Nov.	26	6 56 25
Dec.	7	6 58 50	6 58 02	6 57 12	Dec.	6	6 56 20
Dec.	17	6 58 45	6 57 58	6 57 07	Dec.	16	6 56 15
Dec.	27	6 58 40	6 57 52	6 57 02	Dec.	26	6 56 10
Jan.	6	6 58 35	6 57 47	6 56 57	Jan.	5	6 56 05

SIDEREAL LONGITUDE OF THE VERNAL POINT

Referred to Spica as Fiducial

Date	Common Years 1873	1874	1875	Leap Year 1876	
	° ′ ″	° ′ ″	° ′ ″		° ′ ″
Jan. 1	♓ 56 07	♓ 55 13	♓ 54 18	Jan. 1	♓ 53 23
Jan. 11	6 56 02	6 55 08	6 54 13	Jan. 11	6 53 17
Jan. 21	6 55 56	6 55 03	6 54 08	Jan. 21	6 53 12
Jan. 31	6 55 51	6 54 57	6 54 02	Jan. 31	6 53 07
Feb. 10	6 55 46	6 54 53	6 53 57	Feb. 10	6 53 02
Feb. 20	6 55 42	6 54 48	6 53 53	Feb. 20	6 52 57
Mar. 2	6 55 38	6 54 44	6 53 49	Mar. 1	6 52 54
Mar. 12	6 55 35	6 54 41	6 53 46	Mar. 11	6 52 50
Mar. 22	6 55 33	6 54 38	6 53 43	Mar. 21	6 52 48
Apr. 1	6 55 30	6 54 36	6 53 41	Mar. 31	6 52 45
Apr. 11	6 55 29	6 54 35	6 53 39	Apr. 10	6 52 44
Apr. 21	6 55 28	6 54 34	6 53 38	Apr. 20	6 52 43
May 1	6 55 27	6 54 33	6 53 38	Apr. 30	6 52 42
May 11	6 55 27	6 54 33	6 53 38	May 10	6 52 42
May 21	6 55 27	6 54 33	6 53 38	May 20	6 52 42
May 31	6 55 28	6 54 34	6 53 38	May 30	6 52 42
June 10	6 55 29	6 54 34	6 53 39	June 9	6 52 43
June 20	6 55 30	6 54 36	6 53 40	June 19	6 52 44
June 30	6 55 31	6 54 37	6 53 41	June 29	6 52 45
July 10	6 55 33	6 54 38	6 53 43	July 9	6 52 47
July 20	6 55 34	6 54 40	6 53 44	July 19	6 52 48
July 30	6 55 36	6 54 42	6 53 46	July 29	6 52 50
Aug. 9	6 55 38	6 54 43	6 53 48	Aug. 8	6 52 52
Aug. 19	6 55 39	6 54 45	6 53 49	Aug. 18	6 52 53
Aug. 29	6 55 41	6 54 46	6 53 51	Aug. 28	6 52 55
Sept. 8	6 55 42	6 54 47	6 53 52	Sept. 7	6 52 56
Sept. 18	6 55 43	6 54 48	6 53 53	Sept. 17	6 52 57
Sept. 28	6 55 43	6 54 48	6 53 53	Sept. 27	6 52 57
Oct. 8	6 55 43	6 54 48	6 53 53	Oct. 7	6 52 57
Oct. 18	6 55 42	6 54 47	6 53 52	Oct. 17	6 52 56
Oct. 28	6 55 40	6 54 45	6 53 50	Oct. 27	6 52 54
Nov. 7	6 55 38	6 54 43	6 53 47	Nov. 6	6 52 52
Nov. 17	6 55 35	6 54 40	6 53 44	Nov. 16	6 52 48
Nov. 27	6 55 31	6 54 36	6 53 40	Nov. 26	6 52 44
Dec. 7	6 55 26	6 54 31	6 53 36	Dec. 6	6 52 40
Dec. 17	6 55 21	6 54 26	6 53 31	Dec. 16	6 52 35
Dec. 27	6 55 16	6 54 21	6 53 26	Dec. 26	6 52 30
Jan. 6	6 55 11	6 54 16	6 53 21	Jan. 5	6 52 25

SIDEREAL LONGITUDE OF THE VERNAL POINT

Referred to Spica as Fiducial

Date		Common Years			Leap Year		
		1877	1878	1879			1880
		° ′ ″	° ′ ″	° ′ ″			° ′ ″
Jan.	1	♓ 52 27	♓ 51 31	♓ 50 37	Jan.	1	♓ 49 45
Jan.	11	6 52 21	6 51 26	6 50 32	Jan.	11	6 49 39
Jan.	21	6 52 16	6 51 20	6 50 26	Jan.	21	6 49 34
Jan.	31	6 52 10	6 51 15	6 50 21	Jan.	31	6 49 29
Feb.	10	6 52 06	6 51 10	6 50 16	Feb.	10	6 49 24
Feb.	20	6 52 01	6 51 06	6 50 12	Feb.	20	6 49 20
Mar.	2	6 51 57	6 51 02	6 50 08	Mar.	1	6 49 16
Mar.	12	6 51 54	6 50 59	6 50 05	Mar.	11	6 49 13
Mar.	22	6 51 51	6 50 56	6 50 02	Mar.	21	6 49 10
Apr.	1	6 51 49	6 50 54	6 50 00	Mar.	31	6 49 08
Apr.	11	6 51 48	6 50 53	6 49 59	Apr.	10	6 49 07
Apr.	21	6 51 47	6 50 52	6 49 58	Apr.	20	6 49 06
May	1	6 51 46	6 50 51	6 49 57	Apr.	30	6 49 05
May	11	6 51 46	6 50 51	6 49 57	May	10	6 49 05
May	21	6 51 46	6 50 51	6 49 57	May	20	6 49 05
May	31	6 51 47	6 50 51	6 49 58	May	30	6 49 06
June	10	6 51 47	6 50 52	6 49 59	June	9	6 49 07
June	20	6 51 48	6 50 53	6 50 00	June	19	6 49 08
June	30	6 51 50	6 50 55	6 50 01	June	29	6 49 09
July	10	6 51 51	6 50 56	6 50 03	July	9	6 49 11
July	20	6 51 53	6 50 58	6 50 04	July	19	6 49 13
July	30	6 51 54	6 50 59	6 50 06	July	29	6 49 14
Aug.	9	6 51 56	6 51 01	6 50 08	Aug.	8	6 49 16
Aug.	19	6 51 58	6 51 03	6 50 09	Aug.	18	6 49 18
Aug.	29	6 51 59	6 51 04	6 50 11	Aug.	28	6 49 20
Sept.	8	6 52 00	6 51 05	6 50 12	Sept.	7	6 49 21
Sept.	18	6 52 01	6 51 06	6 50 13	Sept.	17	6 49 22
Sept.	28	6 52 01	6 51 07	6 50 13	Sept.	27	6 49 22
Oct.	8	6 52 01	6 51 06	6 50 13	Oct.	7	6 49 22
Oct.	18	6 52 00	6 51 05	6 50 12	Oct.	17	6 49 21
Oct.	28	6 51 58	6 51 04	6 50 11	Oct.	27	6 49 20
Nov.	7	6 51 56	6 51 01	6 50 08	Nov	6	6 49 18
Nov.	17	6 51 52	6 50 58	6 50 05	Nov.	16	6 49 15
Nov.	27	6 51 49	6 50 54	6 50 02	Nov.	26	6 49 11
Dec.	7	6 51 44	6 50 50	6 59 57	Dec.	6	6 49 07
Dec.	17	6 51 39	6 50 45	6 49 52	Dec.	16	6 49 02
Dec.	27	6 51 34	6 50 40	6 49 47	Dec.	26	6 48 57
Jan.	6	6 51 29	6 50 35	6 49 42	Jan.	5	6 48 52

SIDEREAL LONGITUDE OF THE VERNAL POINT

Referred to Spica as Fiducial

	Common Years			Leap Year	
Date	1881	1882	1883		1884
	° ′ ″	° ′ ″	° ′ ″		° ′ ″
Jan. 1	♓ 48 53	♓ 48 05	♓ 47 18	Jan. 1	♓ 46 32
Jan. 11	6 48 48	6 48 00	6 47 13	Jan. 11	6 46 27
Jan. 21	6 48 43	6 47 54	6 47 08	Jan. 21	6 46 22
Jan. 31	6 48 38	6 47 49	6 47 03	Jan. 31	6 46 17
Feb. 10	6 48 33	6 47 45	6 46 58	Feb. 10	6 46 13
Feb. 20	6 48 29	6 47 41	6 46 54	Feb. 20	6 46 08
Mar. 2	6 48 25	6 47 37	6 46 50	Mar. 1	6 46 05
Mar. 12	6 48 22	6 47 34	6 46 47	Mar. 11	6 46 02
Mar. 22	6 48 20	6 47 31	6 46 45	Mar. 21	6 45 59
Apr. 1	6 48 18	6 47 30	6 46 43	Mar. 31	6 45 57
Apr. 11	6 48 16	6 47 28	6 46 42	Apr. 10	6 45 56
Apr. 21	6 48 15	6 47 27	6 46 41	Apr. 20	6 45 55
May 1	6 48 15	6 47 27	6 46 40	Apr. 30	6 45 55
May 11	6 48 15	6 47 27	6 46 40	May 10	6 45 55
May 21	6 48 15	6 47 27	6 46 41	May 20	6 45 56
May 31	6 48 16	6 47 28	6 46 42	May 30	6 45 56
June 10	6 48 17	6 47 29	6 46 43	June 9	6 45 57
June 20	6 48 18	6 47 30	6 46 44	June 19	6 45 59
June 30	6 48 20	6 47 32	6 46 46	June 29	6 46 00
July 10	6 48 21	6 47 34	6 46 47	July 9	6 46 02
July 20	6 48 23	6 47 35	6 46 49	July 19	6 46 04
July 30	6 48 25	6 47 37	6 46 51	July 29	6 46 06
Aug. 9	6 48 27	6 47 39	6 46 53	Aug. 8	6 46 08
Aug. 19	6 48 29	6 47 41	6 46 55	Aug. 18	6 46 10
Aug. 29	6 48 30	6 47 43	6 46 56	Aug. 28	6 46 11
Sept. 8	6 48 32	6 47 44	6 46 58	Sept. 7	6 46 13
Sept. 18	6 48 33	6 47 45	6 46 59	Sept. 17	6 46 14
Sept. 28	6 48 33	6 47 46	6 47 00	Sept. 27	6 46 15
Oct. 8	6 48 33	6 47 46	6 47 00	Oct. 7	6 46 15
Oct. 18	6 48 32	6 47 45	6 46 59	Oct. 17	6 46 14
Oct. 28	6 48 31	6 47 43	6 46 57	Oct. 27	6 46 13
Nov. 7	6 48 28	6 47 41	6 46 55	Nov. 6	6 46 10
Nov. 17	6 48 25	6 47 38	6 46 52	Nov. 16	6 46 08
Nov. 27	6 48 22	6 47 35	6 46 49	Nov. 26	6 46 04
Dec. 7	6 48 17	6 47 30	6 46 45	Dec. 6	6 46 00
Dec. 17	6 48 12	6 47 25	6 46 40	Dec. 16	6 45 55
Dec. 27	6 48 07	6 47 20	6 46 35	Dec. 26	6 45 50
Jan. 6	6 48 02	6 47 15	6 46 30	Jan. 5	6 45 45

SIDEREAL LONGITUDE OF THE VERNAL POINT

Referred to Spica as Fiducial

Date	Common Years 1885	1886	1887	Leap Year 1888	
	° ′ ″	° ′ ″	° ′ ″		° ′ ″
Jan. 1	♓ 45 47	♓ 45 03	♓ 44 18	Jan. 1	♓ 43 33
Jan. 11	6 45 42	6 44 58	6 44 13	Jan. 11	6 43 28
Jan. 21	6 45 37	6 44 53	6 44 08	Jan. 21	6 43 22
Jan. 31	6 45 32	6 44 48	6 44 03	Jan. 31	6 43 17
Feb. 10	6 45 27	6 44 43	6 43 58	Feb. 10	6 43 13
Feb. 20	6 45 23	6 44 39	6 43 54	Feb. 20	6 43 09
Mar. 2	6 45 20	6 44 36	6 43 51	Mar. 1	6 43 05
Mar. 12	6 45 17	6 44 33	6 43 48	Mar. 11	6 43 02
Mar. 22	6 45 15	6 44 30	6 43 45	Mar. 21	6 43 00
Apr. 1	6 45 13	6 44 28	6 43 43	Mar. 31	6 42 58
Apr. 11	6 45 11	6 44 27	6 43 42	Apr. 10	6 42 56
Apr. 21	6 45 11	6 44 26	6 43 41	Apr. 20	6 42 55
May 1	6 45 10	6 44 26	6 43 41	Apr. 30	6 42 55
May 11	6 45 10	6 44 26	6 43 41	May 10	6 42 55
May 21	6 45 11	6 44 27	6 43 42	May 20	6 42 55
May 31	6 45 12	6 44 27	6 43 42	May 30	6 42 56
June 10	6 45 13	6 44 28	6 43 43	June 9	6 42 57
June 20	6 45 14	6 44 30	6 43 45	June 19	6 42 58
June 30	6 45 16	6 44 31	6 43 46	June 29	6 43 00
July 10	6 45 18	6 44 33	6 43 48	July 9	6 43 02
July 20	6 45 19	6 44 35	6 43 50	July 19	6 43 03
July 30	6 45 21	6 44 37	6 43 52	July 29	6 43 05
Aug. 9	6 45 23	6 44 39	6 43 54	Aug. 8	6 43 07
Aug. 19	6 45 25	6 44 41	6 43 56	Aug. 18	6 43 09
Aug. 29	6 45 27	6 44 43	6 43 57	Aug. 28	6 43 11
Sept. 8	6 45 28	6 44 44	6 43 59	Sept. 7	6 43 12
Sept. 18	6 45 29	6 44 45	6 44 00	Sept. 17	6 43 13
Sept. 28	6 45 29	6 44 46	6 44 00	Sept. 27	6 43 13
Oct. 8	6 45 30	6 44 46	6 44 00	Oct. 7	6 43 13
Oct. 18	6 45 29	6 44 45	6 43 59	Oct. 17	6 43 13
Oct. 28	6 45 28	6 44 44	6 43 58	Oct. 27	6 43 11
Nov. 7	6 45 26	6 44 41	6 43 56	Nov. 6	6 43 09
Nov. 17	6 45 23	6 44 38	6 43 53	Nov. 16	6 43 06
Nov. 27	6 45 19	6 44 35	6 43 49	Nov. 26	6 43 02
Dec. 7	6 45 15	6 44 31	6 43 45	Dec. 6	6 42 58
Dec. 17	6 45 10	6 44 26	6 43 40	Dec. 16	6 42 53
Dec. 27	6 45 05	6 44 21	6 43 35	Dec. 26	6 42 48
Jan. 6	6 45 00	6 44 16	6 43 30	Jan. 5	6 42 43

SIDEREAL LONGITUDE OF THE VERNAL POINT

Referred to Spica as Fiducial

Date		Common Years			Leap Year		
		1889	1890	1891		1892	
		° ′ ″	° ′ ″	° ′ ″			° ′ ″
Jan.	1	♓ 42 45	♓ 41 56	♓ 41 05	Jan.	1	♓ 40 13
Jan.	11	6 42 40	6 41 51	6 41 00	Jan.	11	6 40 07
Jan.	21	6 42 35	6 41 46	6 40 55	Jan.	21	6 40 02
Jan.	31	6 42 30	6 41 41	6 40 49	Jan.	31	6 39 57
Feb.	10	6 42 25	6 41 36	6 40 45	Feb.	10	6 39 52
Feb.	20	6 42 21	6 41 32	6 40 40	Feb.	20	6 39 47
Mar.	2	6 42 17	6 41 28	6 40 37	Mar.	1	6 39 43
Mar.	12	6 42 14	6 41 24	6 40 33	Mar.	11	6 39 40
Mar.	22	6 42 12	6 41 22	6 40 31	Mar.	21	6 39 38
Apr.	1	6 42 10	6 41 20	6 40 29	Mar.	31	6 39 36
Apr.	11	6 42 09	6 41 19	6 40 27	Apr.	10	6 39 34
Apr.	21	6 42 08	6 41 18	6 40 26	Apr.	20	6 39 33
May	1	6 42 07	6 41 17	6 40 26	Apr.	30	6 39 32
May	11	6 42 07	6 41 17	6 40 26	May	10	6 39 32
May	21	6 42 08	6 41 18	6 40 26	May	20	6 39 32
May	31	6 42 08	6 41 18	6 40 26	May	30	6 39 33
June	10	6 42 09	6 41 19	6 40 27	June	9	6 39 34
June	20	6 42 10	6 41 20	6 40 28	June	19	6 39 35
June	30	6 42 12	6 41 22	6 40 30	June	29	6 39 36
July	10	6 42 14	6 41 23	6 40 31	July	9	6 39 38
July	20	6 42 15	6 41 25	6 40 33	July	19	6 39 39
July	30	6 42 17	6 41 27	6 40 35	July	29	6 39 41
Aug.	9	6 42 19	6 41 29	6 40 36	Aug.	8	6 39 43
Aug.	19	6 42 21	6 41 30	6 40 38	Aug.	18	6 39 44
Aug.	29	6 42 22	6 41 32	6 40 40	Aug.	28	6 39 46
Sept.	8	6 42 24	6 41 33	6 40 41	Sept.	7	6 39 47
Sept.	18	6 42 25	6 41 34	6 40 42	Sept.	17	6 39 48
Sept.	28	6 42 25	6 41 34	6 40 42	Sept.	27	6 39 48
Oct.	8	6 42 25	6 41 34	6 40 42	Oct.	7	6 39 48
Oct.	18	6 42 24	6 41 33	6 40 41	Oct.	17	6 39 47
Oct.	28	6 42 22	6 41 32	6 40 39	Oct.	27	6 39 45
Nov.	7	6 42 20	6 41 29	6 40 37	Nov.	6	6 39 43
Nov.	17	6 42 17	6 41 26	6 40 34	Nov.	16	6 39 40
Nov.	27	6 42 13	6 41 22	6 40 30	Nov.	26	6 39 36
Dec.	7	6 42 09	6 41 18	6 40 25	Dec.	6	6 39 31
Dec.	17	6 42 04	6 41 13	6 40 21	Dec.	16	6 39 26
Dec.	27	6 41 59	6 41 08	6 40 15	Dec.	26	6 39 21
Jan.	6	6 41 54	6 41 03	6 40 10	Jan.	5	6 39 16

SIDEREAL LONGITUDE OF THE VERNAL POINT

Referred to Spica as Fiducial

Date		Common Years			Leap Year		
		1893	1894	1895		1896	
		° ′ ″	° ′ ″	° ′ ″			° ′ ″
Jan.	1	♓ 39 18	♓ 38 23	♓ 37 27	Jan.	1	♓ 36 31
Jan.	11	6 39 12	6 38 17	6 37 21	Jan.	11	6 36 26
Jan.	21	6 39 07	6 38 12	6 37 16	Jan.	21	6 36 20
Jan.	31	6 39 02	6 38 07	6 37 11	Jan.	31	6 36 15
Feb.	10	6 38 57	6 38 02	6 37 06	Feb.	10	6 36 10
Feb.	20	6 38 53	6 37 57	6 37 01	Feb.	20	6 36 06
Mar.	2	6 38 49	6 37 53	6 36 58	Mar.	1	6 36 02
Mar.	12	6 38 46	6 37 50	6 36 54	Mar.	11	6 35 59
Mar.	22	6 38 43	6 37 47	6 36 51	Mar.	21	6 35 56
Apr.	1	6 38 41	6 37 45	6 36 49	Mar.	31	6 35 54
Apr.	11	6 38 39	6 37 44	6 36 48	Apr.	10	6 35 52
Apr.	21	6 38 38	6 37 43	6 36 47	Apr.	20	6 35 51
May	1	6 38 38	6 37 42	6 36 46	Apr.	30	6 35 50
May	11	6 38 37	6 37 42	6 36 46	May	10	6 35 50
May	21	6 38 38	6 37 42	6 36 46	May	20	6 35 50
May	31	6 38 38	6 37 43	6 36 46	May	30	6 35 51
June	10	6 38 39	6 37 43	6 36 47	June	9	6 35 52
June	20	6 38 40	6 37 44	6 36 48	June	19	6 35 53
June	30	6 38 41	6 37 46	6 36 49	June	29	6 35 54
July	10	6 38 43	6 37 47	6 36 51	July	9	6 35 55
July	20	6 38 44	6 37 49	6 36 52	July	19	6 35 57
July	30	6 38 46	6 37 50	6 36 54	July	29	6 35 59
Aug.	9	6 38 48	6 37 52	6 36 56	Aug.	8	6 36 00
Aug.	19	6 38 49	6 37 53	6 36 57	Aug.	18	6 36 02
Aug.	29	6 38 51	6 37 55	6 36 59	Aug.	28	6 36 03
Sept.	8	6 38 52	6 37 56	6 37 00	Sept.	7	6 36 04
Sept.	18	6 38 53	6 37 57	6 37 01	Sept.	17	6 36 05
Sept.	28	6 38 53	6 37 57	6 37 01	Sept.	27	6 36 06
Oct.	8	6 38 52	6 37 57	6 37 01	Oct.	7	6 36 05
Oct.	18	6 38 52	6 37 56	6 37 00	Oct.	17	6 36 04
Oct.	28	6 38 50	6 37 54	6 36 58	Oct.	27	6 36 03
Nov.	7	6 38 47	6 37 52	6 36 56	Nov.	6	6 36 00
Nov.	17	6 38 44	6 37 48	6 36 52	Nov.	16	6 35 57
Nov.	27	6 38 40	6 37 44	6 36 48	Nov.	26	6 35 53
Dec.	7	6 38 36	6 37 40	6 36 44	Dec.	6	6 35 49
Dec.	17	6 38 31	6 37 35	6 36 39	Dec.	16	6 35 44
Dec.	27	6 38 25	6 37 30	6 36 34	Dec.	26	6 35 39
Jan.	6	6 38 20	6 37 25	6 36 29	Jan.	5	6 35 34

SIDEREAL LONGITUDE OF THE VERNAL POINT

Referred to Spica as Fiducial

	All Common Years				
Date	1897	1898	1899	\multicolumn{2}{c	}{1900}

Date	1897 ° ′ ″	1898 ° ′ ″	1899 ° ′ ″	Date	1900 ° ′ ″
Jan. 1	♓ 35 36	♓ 34 42	♓ 33 50	Jan. 1	♓ 33 00
Jan. 11	6 35 30	6 34 37	6 33 45	Jan. 11	6 32 55
Jan. 21	6 35 25	6 34 31	6 33 40	Jan. 21	6 32 50
Jan. 31	6 35 20	6 34 26	6 33 35	Jan. 31	6 32 45
Feb. 10	6 35 15	6 34 21	6 33 30	Feb. 10	6 32 40
Feb. 20	6 35 10	6 34 17	6 33 26	Feb. 20	6 32 36
Mar. 2	6 35 06	6 34 13	6 33 22	Mar. 2	6 32 32
Mar. 12	6 35 03	6 34 10	6 33 19	Mar. 12	6 32 29
Mar. 22	6 35 01	6 34 08	6 33 16	Mar. 22	6 32 27
Apr. 1	6 34 59	6 34 06	6 33 14	Apr. 1	6 32 25
Apr. 11	6 34 57	6 34 04	6 33 13	Apr. 11	6 32 23
Apr. 21	6 34 56	6 34 03	6 33 12	Apr. 21	6 32 22
May 1	6 34 56	6 34 03	6 33 11	May 1	6 32 22
May 11	6 34 56	6 34 02	6 33 11	May 11	6 32 22
May 21	6 34 56	6 34 03	6 33 11	May 21	6 32 22
May 31	6 34 56	6 34 03	6 33 12	May 31	6 32 23
June 10	6 34 57	6 34 04	6 33 13	June 10	6 32 24
June 20	6 34 58	6 34 05	6 33 14	June 20	6 32 25
June 30	6 35 00	6 34 07	6 33 16	June 30	6 32 27
July 10	6 35 01	6 34 08	6 33 17	July 10	6 32 28
July 20	6 35 03	6 34 10	6 33 19	July 20	6 32 30
July 30	6 35 04	6 34 12	6 33 21	July 30	6 32 32
Aug. 9	6 35 06	6 34 13	6 33 23	Aug. 9	6 32 34
Aug. 19	6 35 08	6 34 15	6 33 24	Aug. 19	6 32 36
Aug. 29	6 35 09	6 34 16	6 33 26	Aug. 29	6 32 37
Sept. 8	6 35 10	6 34 18	6 33 27	Sept. 8	6 32 39
Sept. 18	6 35 11	6 34 19	6 33 28	Sept. 18	6 32 40
Sept. 28	6 35 12	6 34 19	6 33 29	Sept. 28	6 32 40
Oct. 8	6 35 11	6 34 19	6 33 29	Oct. 8	6 32 40
Oct. 18	6 35 10	6 34 18	6 33 28	Oct. 18	6 32 39
Oct. 28	6 35 09	6 34 17	6 33 26	Oct. 28	6 32 38
Nov. 7	6 35 06	6 34 14	6 33 24	Nov. 7	6 32 36
Nov. 17	6 35 03	6 34 11	6 33 21	Nov. 17	6 32 33
Nov. 27	6 34 59	6 34 07	6 33 17	Nov. 27	6 32 29
Dec. 7	6 34 55	6 34 03	6 33 13	Dec. 7	6 32 25
Dec. 17	6 34 50	6 33 58	6 44 08	Dec. 17	6 32 20
Dec. 27	6 34 45	6 33 53	6 33 03	Dec. 27	6 32 15
Jan. 6	6 34 40	6 33 48	6 32 58	Jan. 6	6 32 10

SIDEREAL LONGITUDE OF THE VERNAL POINT

Referred to Spica as Fiducial

Date	Common Years 1901	1902	1903	Leap Year Date	1904
	° ′ ″	° ′ ″	° ′ ″		° ′ ″
Jan. 1	♓ 32 13	♓ 31 26	♓ 30 41	Jan. 1	♓ 29 57
Jan. 11	6 32 07	6 31 21	6 30 36	Jan. 11	6 29 51
Jan. 21	6 32 02	6 31 16	6 30 31	Jan. 21	6 29 46
Jan. 31	6 31 57	6 31 11	6 30 26	Jan. 31	6 29 41
Feb. 10	6 31 53	6 31 06	6 30 21	Feb. 10	6 29 37
Feb. 20	6 31 48	6 31 02	6 30 17	Feb. 20	6 29 33
Mar. 2	6 31 45	6 30 59	6 30 14	Mar. 1	6 29 29
Mar. 12	6 31 42	6 30 56	6 30 11	Mar. 11	6 29 26
Mar. 22	6 31 39	6 30 53	6 30 08	Mar. 21	6 29 24
Apr. 1	6 31 37	6 30 51	6 30 06	Mar. 31	6 29 22
Apr. 11	6 31 36	6 30 50	6 30 05	Apr. 10	6 29 21
Apr. 21	6 31 35	6 30 49	6 30 04	Apr. 20	6 29 20
May 1	6 31 35	6 30 49	6 30 04	Apr. 30	6 29 20
May 11	6 31 35	6 30 49	6 30 04	May 10	6 29 20
May 21	6 31 36	6 30 50	6 30 05	May 20	6 29 20
May 31	6 31 36	6 30 50	6 30 05	May 30	6 29 21
June 10	6 31 37	6 30 51	6 30 06	June 9	6 29 22
June 20	6 31 39	6 30 53	6 30 08	June 19	6 29 23
June 30	6 31 40	6 30 54	6 30 09	June 29	6 29 25
July 10	6 31 42	6 30 56	6 30 11	July 9	6 29 27
July 20	6 31 44	6 30 58	6 30 13	July 19	6 29 29
July 30	6 31 46	6 31 00	6 30 15	July 29	6 29 30
Aug. 9	6 31 48	6 31 02	6 30 17	Aug. 8	6 29 32
Aug. 19	6 31 49	6 31 04	6 30 19	Aug. 18	6 29 34
Aug. 29	6 31 51	6 31 05	6 30 21	Aug. 28	6 29 36
Sept. 8	6 31 52	6 31 07	6 30 22	Sept. 7	6 29 38
Sept. 18	6 31 53	6 31 08	6 30 23	Sept. 17	6 29 39
Sept. 28	6 31 54	6 31 08	6 30 24	Sept. 27	6 29 39
Oct. 8	6 31 54	6 31 08	6 30 24	Oct. 7	6 29 39
Oct. 18	6 31 53	6 31 08	6 30 23	Oct. 17	6 29 39
Oct. 28	6 31 52	6 31 06	6 30 22	Oct. 27	6 29 37
Nov. 7	6 31 49	6 31 04	6 30 20	Nov. 6	6 29 35
Nov. 17	6 31 46	6 31 01	6 30 17	Nov. 16	6 29 32
Nov. 27	6 31 43	6 30 57	6 30 13	Nov. 26	6 29 29
Dec. 7	6 31 39	6 30 53	6 30 09	Dec. 6	6 29 25
Dec. 17	6 31 34	6 30 49	6 30 04	Dec. 16	6 29 20
Dec. 27	6 31 29	6 30 44	6 29 59	Dec. 26	6 29 15
Jan. 6	6 31 24	6 30 39	6 29 54	Jan. 5	6 29 10

SIDEREAL LONGITUDE OF THE VERNAL POINT

Referred to Spica as Fiducial

Date	Common Years 1905	1906	1907	Leap Year 1908	
	° ′ ″	° ′ ″	° ′ ″		° ′ ″
Jan. 1	♓ 29 12	♓ 28 27	♓ 27 41	Jan. 1	♓ 26 53
Jan. 11	6 29 07	6 28 22	6 27 35	Jan. 11	6 26 48
Jan. 21	6 29 02	6 28 17	6 27 30	Jan. 21	6 26 42
Jan. 31	6 28 57	6 28 12	6 27 25	Jan. 31	6 26 37
Feb. 10	6 28 52	6 28 07	6 27 21	Feb. 10	6 26 33
Feb. 20	6 28 48	6 28 03	6 27 17	Feb. 20	6 26 29
Mar. 2	6 28 44	6 27 59	6 27 13	Mar. 1	6 26 25
Mar. 12	6 28 41	6 27 56	6 27 10	Mar. 11	6 26 22
Mar. 22	6 28 39	6 27 54	6 27 07	Mar. 21	6 26 19
Apr. 1	6 28 37	6 27 52	6 27 05	Mar. 31	6 26 17
Apr. 11	6 28 36	6 27 51	6 27 04	Apr. 10	6 26 16
Apr. 21	6 28 35	6 27 50	6 27 03	Apr. 20	6 26 15
May 1	6 28 35	6 27 50	6 27 03	Apr. 30	6 26 14
May 11	6 28 35	6 27 50	6 27 03	May 10	6 26 14
May 21	6 28 36	6 27 50	6 27 03	May 20	6 26 15
May 31	6 28 36	6 27 51	6 27 04	May 30	6 26 15
June 10	6 28 37	6 27 52	6 27 05	June 9	6 26 16
June 20	6 28 39	6 27 53	6 27 06	June 19	6 26 17
June 30	6 28 40	6 27 55	6 27 08	June 29	6 26 19
July 10	6 28 42	6 27 56	6 27 09	July 9	6 26 20
July 20	6 28 44	6 27 58	6 27 11	July 19	6 26 22
July 30	6 28 46	6 28 00	6 27 13	July 29	6 26 24
Aug. 9	6 28 48	6 28 02	6 27 15	Aug. 8	6 26 26
Aug. 19	6 28 50	6 28 04	6 27 17	Aug. 18	6 26 27
Aug. 29	6 28 51	6 28 06	6 27 18	Aug. 28	6 26 29
Sept. 8	6 28 53	6 28 07	6 27 20	Sept. 7	6 26 30
Sept. 18	6 28 54	6 28 08	6 27 20	Sept. 17	6 26 31
Sept. 28	6 28 54	6 28 09	6 27 21	Sept. 27	6 26 32
Oct. 8	6 28 54	6 28 09	6 27 21	Oct. 7	6 26 32
Oct. 18	6 28 54	6 28 08	6 27 20	Oct. 17	6 26 31
Oct. 28	6 28 52	6 28 06	6 27 19	Oct. 27	6 26 29
Nov. 7	6 28 50	6 28 04	6 27 17	Nov. 6	6 26 27
Nov. 17	6 28 47	6 28 01	6 27 14	Nov. 16	6 26 24
Nov. 27	6 28 43	6 27 57	6 27 10	Nov. 26	6 26 20
Dec. 7	6 28 39	6 27 53	6 27 06	Dec. 6	6 26 16
Dec. 17	6 28 35	6 27 48	6 27 01	Dec. 16	6 26 11
Dec. 27	6 28 30	6 27 43	6 26 56	Dec. 26	6 26 06
Jan. 6	6 28 25	6 27 38	6 26 51	Jan. 5	6 26 01

SIDEREAL LONGITUDE OF THE VERNAL POINT

Referred to Spica as Fiducial

Date	Common Years 1909	1910	1911	Date	Leap Year 1912
	° ′ ″	° ′ ″	° ′ ″		° ′ ″
Jan. 1	♓ 26 03	♓ 25 11	♓ 24 18	Jan. 1	♓ 23 23
Jan. 11	6 25 57	6 25 06	6 24 12	Jan. 11	6 23 18
Jan. 21	6 25 52	6 25 00	6 24 07	Jan. 21	6 23 12
Jan. 31	6 25 47	6 24 55	6 24 02	Jan. 31	6 23 07
Feb. 10	6 25 42	6 24 50	6 23 57	Feb. 10	6 23 02
Feb. 20	6 25 38	6 24 46	6 23 53	Feb. 20	6 22 58
Mar. 2	6 25 34	6 24 42	6 23 49	Mar. 1	6 22 54
Mar. 12	6 25 31	6 24 39	6 23 45	Mar. 11	6 22 51
Mar. 22	6 25 29	6 24 37	6 23 43	Mar. 21	6 22 48
Apr. 1	6 25 27	6 24 35	6 23 41	Mar. 31	6 22 46
Apr. 11	6 25 25	6 24 33	6 23 39	Apr. 10	6 22 44
Apr. 21	6 25 24	6 24 32	6 23 37	Apr. 20	6 22 43
May 1	6 25 24	6 24 31	6 23 36	Apr. 30	6 22 42
May 11	6 25 24	6 24 31	6 23 37	May 10	6 22 42
May 21	6 25 24	6 24 32	6 23 37	May 20	6 22 42
May 31	6 25 25	6 24 32	6 23 38	May 30	6 22 43
June 10	6 25 26	6 24 33	6 23 39	June 9	6 22 44
June 20	6 25 27	6 24 34	6 23 40	June 19	6 22 45
June 30	6 25 28	6 24 35	6 23 41	June 29	6 22 46
July 10	6 25 30	6 24 37	6 23 43	July 9	6 22 47
July 20	6 25 31	6 24 39	6 23 44	July 19	6 22 49
July 30	6 25 33	6 24 40	6 23 46	July 29	6 22 51
Aug. 9	6 25 35	6 24 42	6 23 48	Aug. 8	6 22 52
Aug. 19	6 25 37	6 24 44	6 23 49	Aug. 18	6 22 54
Aug. 29	6 25 38	6 24 45	6 23 51	Aug. 28	6 22 55
Sept. 8	6 25 39	6 24 46	6 23 52	Sept. 7	6 22 56
Sept. 18	6 25 40	6 24 47	6 23 53	Sept. 17	6 22 57
Sept. 28	6 25 40	6 24 47	6 23 53	Sept. 27	6 22 57
Oct. 8	6 25 40	6 24 47	6 23 53	Oct. 7	6 22 57
Oct. 18	6 25 39	6 24 46	6 23 52	Oct. 17	6 22 56
Oct. 28	6 25 38	6 24 45	6 23 50	Oct. 27	6 22 55
Nov. 7	6 25 35	6 24 42	6 23 48	Nov. 6	6 22 52
Nov. 17	6 25 32	6 24 39	6 23 44	Nov. 16	6 22 49
Nov. 27	6 25 28	6 24 35	6 23 40	Nov. 26	6 22 45
Dec. 7	6 25 24	6 24 31	6 23 36	Dec. 6	6 22 41
Dec. 17	6 25 19	6 24 26	6 23 31	Dec. 16	6 22 36
Dec. 27	6 25 14	6 24 20	6 23 26	Dec. 26	6 22 30
Jan. 6	6 25 09	6 24 15	6 23 21	Jan. 5	6 22 25

SIDEREAL LONGITUDE OF THE VERNAL POINT

Referred to Spica as Fiducial

Date	Common Years 1913	1914	1915	Leap Year 1916	
	° ′ ″	° ′ ″	° ′ ″		° ′ ″
Jan. 1	♓ 22 27	♓ 21 31	♓ 20 36	Jan. 1	♓ 19 41
Jan. 11	6 22 22	6 21 26	6 20 30	Jan. 11	6 19 36
Jan. 21	6 22 16	6 21 20	6 20 25	Jan. 21	6 19 30
Jan. 31	6 22 11	6 21 15	6 20 20	Jan. 31	6 19 25
Feb. 10	6 22 06	6 21 10	6 20 15	Feb. 10	6 19 20
Feb. 20	6 22 02	6 21 06	6 20 10	Feb. 20	6 19 16
Mar. 2	6 21 58	6 21 02	6 20 06	Mar. 1	6 19 12
Mar. 12	6 21 55	6 20 59	6 20 03	Mar. 11	6 19 09
Mar. 22	6 21 52	6 20 56	6 20 00	Mar. 21	6 19 06
Apr. 1	6 21 50	6 20 54	6 19 58	Mar. 31	6 19 04
Apr. 11	6 21 48	6 20 52	6 19 57	Apr. 10	6 19 03
Apr. 21	6 21 47	6 20 51	6 19 56	Apr. 20	6 19 02
May 1	6 21 47	6 20 51	6 19 55	Apr. 30	6 19 01
May 11	6 21 46	6 20 50	6 19 55	May 10	6 19 01
May 21	6 21 47	6 20 50	6 19 55	May 20	6 19 01
May 31	6 21 47	6 20 51	6 19 56	May 30	6 19 02
June 10	6 21 48	6 20 52	6 19 57	June 9	6 19 03
June 20	6 21 49	6 20 53	6 19 58	June 19	6 19 04
June 30	6 21 50	6 20 54	6 19 59	June 29	6 19 05
July 10	6 21 52	6 20 55	6 20 00	July 9	6 19 06
July 20	6 21 53	6 20 57	6 20 02	July 19	6 19 08
July 30	6 21 55	6 20 59	6 20 04	July 29	6 19 10
Aug. 9	6 21 56	6 21 00	6 20 05	Aug. 8	6 19 12
Aug. 19	6 21 58	6 21 02	6 20 07	Aug. 18	6 19 13
Aug. 29	6 21 59	6 21 04	6 20 08	Aug. 28	6 19 15
Sept. 8	6 22 00	6 21 05	6 20 10	Sept. 7	6 19 16
Sept. 18	6 22 01	6 21 05	6 20 10	Sept. 17	6 19 17
Sept. 28	6 22 01	6 21 06	6 20 11	Sept. 27	6 19 17
Oct. 8	6 22 01	6 21 05	6 20 10	Oct. 7	6 19 17
Oct. 18	6 22 00	6 21 04	6 20 10	Oct. 17	6 19 16
Oct. 28	6 21 58	6 21 03	6 20 08	Oct. 27	6 19 15
Nov. 7	6 21 56	6 21 00	6 20 05	Nov. 6	6 19 12
Nov. 17	6 21 53	6 20 57	6 20 02	Nov. 16	6 19 09
Nov. 27	6 21 50	6 20 53	6 19 59	Nov. 26	6 19 05
Dec. 7	6 21 44	6 20 49	6 19 54	Dec. 6	6 19 01
Dec. 17	6 21 39	6 20 44	6 19 49	Dec. 16	6 18 56
Dec. 27	6 21 34	6 20 38	6 19 44	Dec. 26	6 18 51
Jan. 6	6 21 29	6 20 33	6 19 39	Jan. 5	6 18 46

SIDEREAL LONGITUDE OF THE VERNAL POINT

Referred to Spica as Fiducial

Date	Common Years 1917	1918	1919	Leap Year 1920	
	° ′ ″	° ′ ″	° ′ ″		° ′ ″
Jan. 1	♓ 18 48	♓ 17 57	♓ 17 08	Jan. 1	♓ 16 20
Jan. 11	6 18 42	6 17 51	6 17 02	Jan. 11	6 16 15
Jan. 21	6 18 37	6 17 46	6 16 57	Jan. 21	6 16 10
Jan. 31	6 18 32	6 17 41	6 16 52	Jan. 31	6 16 05
Feb. 10	6 18 27	6 17 36	6 16 47	Feb. 10	6 16 00
Feb. 20	6 18 23	6 17 32	6 16 43	Feb. 20	6 15 56
Mar. 2	6 18 19	6 17 28	6 16 40	Mar. 1	6 15 53
Mar. 12	6 18 16	6 17 25	6 16 37	Mar. 11	6 15 50
Mar. 22	6 18 14	6 17 23	6 16 34	Mar. 21	6 15 47
Apr. 1	6 18 12	6 17 21	6 16 32	Mar. 31	6 15 45
Apr. 11	6 18 10	6 17 20	6 16 31	Apr. 10	6 15 44
Apr. 21	6 18 09	6 17 19	6 16 30	Apr. 20	6 15 43
May 1	6 18 09	6 17 18	6 16 30	Apr. 30	6 15 43
May 11	6 18 08	6 17 18	6 16 30	May 10	6 15 43
May 21	6 18 09	6 17 18	6 16 30	May 20	6 15 43
May 31	6 18 09	6 17 19	6 16 31	May 30	6 15 44
June 10	6 18 10	6 17 20	6 16 32	June 9	6 15 45
June 20	6 18 12	6 17 21	6 16 33	June 19	6 15 46
June 30	6 18 13	6 17 23	6 16 34	June 29	6 15 48
July 10	6 18 15	6 17 24	6 16 36	July 9	6 15 49
July 20	6 18 16	6 17 26	6 16 38	July 19	6 15 51
July 30	6 18 18	6 17 28	6 16 40	July 29	6 15 53
Aug. 9	6 18 20	6 17 30	6 16 42	Aug. 8	6 15 55
Aug. 19	6 18 22	6 17 31	6 16 43	Aug. 18	6 15 57
Aug. 29	6 18 23	6 17 33	6 16 45	Aug. 28	6 15 59
Sept. 8	6 18 24	6 17 34	6 16 46	Sept. 7	6 16 00
Sept. 18	6 18 25	6 17 35	6 16 47	Sept. 17	6 16 01
Sept. 28	6 18 26	6 17 36	6 16 48	Sept. 27	6 16 02
Oct. 8	6 18 25	6 17 35	6 16 48	Oct. 7	6 16 02
Oct. 18	6 18 25	6 17 35	6 16 47	Oct. 17	6 16 01
Oct. 28	6 18 23	6 17 33	6 16 46	Oct. 27	6 16 00
Nov. 7	6 18 21	6 17 31	6 16 44	Nov. 6	6 15 58
Nov. 17	6 18 18	6 17 28	6 16 41	Nov. 16	6 15 55
Nov. 27	6 18 14	6 17 24	6 16 37	Nov. 26	6 15 51
Dec. 7	6 18 09	6 17 20	6 16 33	Dec. 6	6 15 47
Dec. 17	6 18 04	6 17 15	6 16 28	Dec. 16	6 15 42
Dec. 27	6 17 59	6 17 10	6 16 23	Dec. 26	6 15 37
Jan. 6	6 17 54	6 17 05	6 16 18	Jan. 5	6 15 32

SIDEREAL LONGITUDE OF THE VERNAL POINT

Referred to Spica as Fiducial

Date	Common Years 1921	1922	1923	Leap Year 1924	
	° ′ ″	° ′ ″	° ′ ″		° ′ ″
Jan. 1	♓ 15 34	♓ 14 49	♓ 14 05	Jan. 1	♓ 13 21
Jan. 11	6 15 29	6 14 44	6 14 00	Jan. 11	6 13 15
Jan. 21	6 15 24	6 14 39	6 13 55	Jan. 21	6 13 10
Jan. 31	6 15 19	6 14 34	6 13 50	Jan. 31	6 13 05
Feb. 10	6 15 14	6 14 29	6 13 45	Feb. 10	6 13 01
Feb. 20	6 15 10	6 14 25	6 13 41	Feb. 20	6 12 57
Mar. 2	6 15 07	6 14 22	6 13 38	Mar. 1	6 12 53
Mar. 12	6 15 04	6 14 19	6 13 35	Mar. 11	6 12 50
Mar. 22	6 15 01	6 14 16	6 13 32	Mar. 21	6 12 48
Apr. 1	6 14 59	6 14 14	6 13 30	Mar. 31	6 12 46
Apr. 11	6 14 58	6 14 13	6 13 29	Apr. 10	6 12 44
Apr. 21	6 14 57	6 14 13	6 13 28	Apr. 20	6 12 44
May 1	6 14 57	6 14 12	6 13 28	Apr. 30	6 12 43
May 11	6 14 57	6 14 12	6 13 28	May 10	6 12 43
May 21	6 14 58	6 14 13	6 13 28	May 20	6 12 44
May 31	6 14 58	6 14 14	6 13 29	May 30	6 12 44
June 10	6 14 59	6 14 15	6 13 30	June 9	6 12 46
June 30	6 15 01	6 14 16	6 13 32	June 19	6 12 47
June 30	6 15 02	6 14 18	6 13 33	June 29	6 12 48
July 10	6 15 04	6 14 19	6 13 35	July 9	6 12 50
July 20	6 15 06	6 14 21	6 13 37	July 19	6 12 52
July 30	6 15 08	6 14 23	6 13 39	July 29	6 12 54
Aug. 9	6 15 10	6 14 25	6 13 41	Aug. 8	6 12 56
Aug. 19	6 15 12	6 14 27	6 13 43	Aug. 18	6 12 58
Aug. 29	6 15 13	6 14 29	6 13 44	Aug. 28	6 12 59
Sept. 8	6 15 15	6 14 30	6 13 46	Sept. 7	6 13 01
Sept. 18	6 15 16	6 14 31	6 13 47	Sept. 17	6 13 02
Sept. 28	6 15 17	6 14 32	6 13 48	Sept. 27	6 13 02
Oct. 8	6 15 17	6 14 32	6 13 48	Oct. 7	6 13 02
Oct. 18	6 15 16	6 14 31	6 13 47	Oct. 17	6 13 02
Oct. 28	6 15 14	6 14 30	6 13 46	Oct. 27	6 13 00
Nov. 7	6 15 12	6 14 28	6 13 43	Nov. 6	6 12 58
Nov. 17	6 15 09	6 14 25	6 13 40	Nov. 16	6 12 55
Nov. 27	6 15 06	6 14 21	6 13 37	Nov. 26	6 12 52
Dec. 7	6 15 02	6 14 17	6 13 33	Dec. 6	6 12 48
Dec. 17	6 14 57	6 14 12	6 13 28	Dec. 16	6 12 43
Dec. 27	6 14 52	6 14 07	6 13 23	Dec. 26	6 12 38
Jan. 6	6 14 47	6 14 02	6 13 18	Jan. 5	6 12 33

SIDEREAL LONGITUDE OF THE VERNAL POINT

Referred to Spica as Fiducial

Date	Common Years 1925	1926	1927	Leap Year 1928	
	° ′ ″	° ′ ″	° ′ ″		° ′ ″
Jan. 1	♓ 12 35	♓ 11 48	♓ 10 59	Jan. 1	♓ 10 09
Jan. 11	6 12 29	6 11 43	6 10 54	Jan. 11	6 10 04
Jan. 21	6 12 24	6 11 37	6 10 49	Jan. 21	6 09 58
Jan. 31	6 12 19	6 11 32	6 10 44	Jan. 31	6 09 53
Feb. 10	6 12 15	6 11 28	6 10 39	Feb. 10	6 09 48
Feb. 20	6 12 11	6 11 24	6 10 35	Feb. 20	6 09 44
Mar. 2	6 12 07	6 11 20	6 10 31	Mar. 1	6 09 40
Mar. 12	6 12 04	6 11 17	6 10 28	Mar. 11	6 09 37
Mar. 22	6 12 02	6 11 15	6 10 25	Mar. 21	6 09 34
Apr. 1	6 12 00	6 11 13	6 10 23	Mar. 31	6 09 32
Apr. 11	6 11 59	6 11 11	6 10 22	Apr. 10	6 09 31
Apr. 21	6 11 58	6 11 10	6 10 21	Apr. 20	6 09 30
May 1	6 11 57	6 11 10	6 10 21	Apr. 30	6 09 29
May 11	6 11 57	6 11 10	6 10 21	May 10	6 09 29
May 21	6 11 58	6 11 10	6 10 21	May 20	6 09 30
May 31	6 11 59	6 11 11	6 10 22	May 30	6 09 30
June 10	6 12 00	6 11 12	6 10 23	June 9	6 09 31
June 20	6 12 01	6 11 13	6 10 24	June 19	6 09 32
June 30	6 12 02	6 11 15	6 10 25	June 29	6 09 33
July 10	6 12 04	6 11 16	6 10 26	July 9	6 09 35
July 20	6 12 06	6 11 18	6 10 28	July 19	6 09 37
July 30	6 12 08	6 11 20	6 10 30	July 29	6 09 38
Aug. 9	6 12 10	6 11 22	6 10 32	Aug. 8	6 09 40
Aug. 19	6 12 12	6 11 24	6 10 34	Aug. 18	6 09 41
Aug. 29	6 12 13	6 11 25	6 10 35	Aug. 28	6 09 43
Sept. 8	6 12 15	6 11 26	6 10 36	Sept. 7	6 09 44
Sept. 18	6 12 16	6 11 27	6 10 37	Sept. 17	6 09 45
Sept. 28	6 12 16	6 11 28	6 10 38	Sept. 27	6 09 46
Oct. 8	6 12 16	6 11 28	6 10 38	Oct. 7	6 09 46
Oct. 18	6 12 15	6 11 27	6 10 37	Oct. 17	6 09 45
Oct. 28	6 12 14	6 11 25	6 10 35	Oct. 27	6 09 43
Nov. 7	6 12 11	6 11 23	6 10 33	Nov. 6	6 09 41
Nov. 17	6 12 08	6 11 20	6 10 30	Nov. 16	6 09 38
Nov. 27	6 12 05	6 11 16	6 10 26	Nov. 26	6 09 34
Dec. 7	6 12 01	6 11 12	6 10 22	Dec. 6	6 09 29
Dec. 17	6 11 56	6 11 07	6 10 17	Dec. 16	6 09 24
Dec. 27	6 11 51	6 11 02	6 10 12	Dec. 26	6 09 19
Jan. 6	6 11 46	6 10 57	6 10 07	Jan. 5	6 09 14

SIDEREAL LONGITUDE OF THE VERNAL POINT

Referred to Spica as Fiducial

	Common Years			Leap Year	
Date	1929	1930	1931	1932	
	° ′ ″	° ′ ″	° ′ ″		° ′ ″
Jan. 1	♓ 09 16	♓ 08 22	♓ 07 27	Jan. 1	♓ 06 32
Jan. 11	6 09 11	6 08 17	6 07 22	Jan. 11	6 06 26
Jan. 21	6 09 05	6 08 11	6 07 16	Jan. 21	6 06 21
Jan. 31	6 09 00	6 08 06	6 07 11	Jan. 31	6 06 16
Feb. 10	6 08 55	6 08 01	6 07 06	Feb. 10	6 06 11
Feb. 20	6 08 51	6 07 57	6 07 02	Feb. 20	6 06 06
Mar. 2	6 08 47	6 07 53	6 06 58	Mar. 1	6 06 02
Mar. 12	6 08 44	6 07 50	6 06 55	Mar. 11	6 05 59
Mar. 22	6 08 41	6 07 47	6 06 52	Mar. 21	6 05 56
Apr. 1	6 08 39	6 07 45	6 06 50	Mar. 31	6 05 54
Apr. 11	6 08 38	6 07 44	6 06 48	Apr. 10	6 05 52
Apr. 21	6 08 37	6 07 43	6 06 47	Apr. 20	6 05 51
May 1	6 08 36	6 07 42	6 06 46	Apr. 30	6 05 51
May 11	6 08 36	6 07 42	6 06 46	May 10	6 05 50
May 21	6 08 36	6 07 42	6 06 46	May 20	6 05 50
May 31	6 08 37	6 07 42	6 06 47	May 30	6 05 51
June 10	6 08 38	6 07 43	6 06 48	June 9	6 05 52
June 20	6 08 39	6 07 44	6 06 49	June 19	6 05 53
June 30	6 08 40	6 07 46	6 06 50	June 29	6 05 54
July 10	6 08 42	6 07 47	6 06 51	July 9	6 05 55
July 20	6 08 43	6 07 49	6 06 53	July 19	6 05 57
July 30	6 08 45	6 07 51	6 06 55	July 29	6 05 59
Aug. 9	6 08 47	6 07 52	6 06 56	Aug. 8	6 06 00
Aug. 19	6 08 48	6 07 54	6 06 58	Aug. 18	6 06 02
Aug. 29	6 08 50	6 07 55	6 06 59	Aug. 28	6 06 03
Sept. 8	6 08 51	6 07 56	6 07 00	Sept. 7	6 06 04
Sept. 18	6 08 52	6 07 57	6 07 01	Sept. 17	6 06 05
Sept. 28	6 08 52	6 07 57	6 07 01	Sept. 27	6 06 05
Oct. 8	6 08 52	6 07 57	6 07 01	Oct. 7	6 06 05
Oct. 18	6 08 51	6 07 56	6 07 00	Oct. 17	6 06 04
Oct. 28	6 08 49	6 07 54	6 06 59	Oct. 27	6 06 02
Nov. 7	6 08 47	6 07 52	6 06 56	Nov. 6	6 06 00
Nov. 17	6 08 44	6 07 49	6 06 53	Nov. 16	6 05 57
Nov. 27	6 08 40	6 07 45	6 06 49	Nov. 26	6 05 53
Dec. 7	6 08 35	6 07 40	6 06 44	Dec. 6	6 05 49
Dec. 17	6 08 30	6 07 35	6 06 39	Dec. 16	6 05 44
Dec. 27	6 08 25	6 07 30	6 06 34	Dec. 26	6 05 38
Jan. 6	6 08 20	6 07 25	6 06 29	Jan. 5	6 05 33

SIDEREAL LONGITUDE OF THE VERNAL POINT

Referred to Spica as Fiducial

Date	Common Years 1933	1934	1935	Leap Year 1936	
	° ′ ″	° ′ ″	° ′ ″		° ′ ″
Jan. 1	♓ 05 35	♓ 04 40	♓ 03 46	Jan. 1	♓ 02 54
Jan. 11	6 05 30	6 04 34	6 03 41	Jan. 11	6 02 48
Jan. 21	6 05 24	6 04 29	6 03 35	Jan. 21	6 02 43
Jan. 31	6 05 19	6 04 24	6 03 30	Jan. 31	6 02 38
Feb. 10	6 05 14	6 04 19	6 03 25	Feb. 10	6 02 33
Feb. 20	6 05 10	6 04 15	6 03 21	Feb. 20	6 02 29
Mar. 2	6 05 06	6 04 11	6 03 17	Mar. 1	6 02 25
Mar. 12	6 05 03	6 04 08	6 03 14	Mar. 11	6 02 22
Mar. 22	6 05 00	6 04 05	6 03 11	Mar. 21	6 02 19
Apr. 1	6 04 58	6 04 03	6 03 09	Mar. 31	6 02 17
Apr. 11	6 04 56	6 04 01	6 03 08	Apr. 10	6 02 16
Apr. 21	6 04 55	6 04 00	6 03 07	Apr. 20	6 02 15
May 1	6 04 55	6 04 00	6 03 06	Apr. 30	6 02 14
May 11	6 04 54	6 04 00	6 03 06	May 10	6 02 14
May 21	6 04 55	6 04 00	6 03 06	May 20	6 02 15
May 31	6 04 55	6 04 00	6 03 07	May 30	6 02 15
June 10	6 04 56	6 04 01	6 03 08	June 9	6 02 16
June 20	6 04 57	6 04 02	6 03 09	June 19	6 02 17
June 30	6 04 58	6 04 03	6 03 10	June 29	6 02 19
July 10	6 05 00	6 04 05	6 03 12	July 9	6 02 20
July 20	6 05 01	6 04 07	6 03 13	July 19	6 02 22
July 30	6 05 03	6 04 08	6 03 15	July 29	6 02 24
Aug. 9	6 05 05	6 04 10	6 03 17	Aug. 8	6 02 26
Aug. 19	6 05 06	6 04 12	6 03 19	Aug. 18	6 02 27
Aug. 29	6 05 08	6 04 13	6 03 20	Aug. 28	6 02 29
Sept. 8	6 05 09	6 04 14	6 03 21	Sept. 7	6 02 30
Sept. 18	6 05 10	6 04 15	6 03 22	Sept. 17	6 02 31
Sept. 28	6 05 10	6 04 15	6 03 23	Sept. 27	6 02 32
Oct. 8	6 05 10	6 04 15	6 03 22	Oct. 7	6 02 32
Oct. 18	6 05 09	6 04 14	6 03 21	Oct. 17	6 02 31
Oct. 28	6 05 07	6 04 13	6 03 20	Oct. 27	6 02 29
Nov. 7	6 05 04	6 04 10	6 03 18	Nov. 6	6 02 27
Nov. 17	6 05 01	6 04 07	6 03 15	Nov. 16	6 02 24
Nov. 27	6 04 57	6 04 03	6 03 11	Nov. 26	6 02 20
Dec. 7	6 04 53	6 03 59	6 03 06	Dec. 6	6 02 16
Dec. 17	6 04 48	6 03 54	6 03 02	Dec. 16	6 02 11
Dec. 27	6 04 43	6 03 49	6 02 56	Dec. 26	6 02 06
Jan. 6	6 04 38	6 03 44	6 02 51	Jan. 5	6 02 01

SIDEREAL LONGITUDE OF THE VERNAL POINT

Referred to Spica as Fiducial

Date	Common Years 1937	1938	1939	Leap Year 1940	
	° ′ ″	° ′ ″	° ′ ″		° ′ ″
Jan. 1	♓ 02 03	♓ 01 15	♓ 00 28	Jan. 1	♓ 59 42
Jan. 11	6 01 58	6 01 09	6 00 23	Jan. 11	5 59 37
Jan. 21	6 01 52	6 01 04	6 00 17	Jan. 21	5 59 32
Jan. 31	6 01 47	6 00 59	6 00 12	Jan. 31	5 59 27
Feb. 10	6 01 43	6 00 54	6 00 08	Feb. 10	5 59 22
Feb. 20	6 01 39	6 00 50	6 00 04	Feb. 20	5 59 18
Mar. 2	6 01 35	6 00 47	6 00 00	Mar. 1	5 59 14
Mar. 12	6 01 32	6 00 44	5 59 57	Mar. 11	5 59 11
Mar. 22	6 01 29	6 00 41	5 59 55	Mar. 21	5 59 09
Apr. 1	6 01 27	6 00 39	5 59 53	Mar. 31	5 59 07
Apr. 11	6 01 26	6 00 38	5 59 52	Apr. 10	5 59 06
Apr. 21	6 01 25	6 00 37	5 59 51	Apr. 20	5 59 05
May 1	6 01 25	6 00 37	5 59 51	Apr. 30	5 59 05
May 11	6 01 25	6 00 37	5 59 51	May 10	5 59 05
May 21	6 01 25	6 00 37	5 59 51	May 20	5 59 05
May 31	6 01 26	6 00 38	5 59 52	May 30	5 59 06
June 10	6 01 27	6 00 39	5 59 53	June 9	5 59 07
June 20	6 01 28	6 00 40	5 59 54	June 19	5 59 09
June 30	6 01 29	6 00 42	5 59 56	June 29	5 59 10
July 10	6 01 31	6 00 43	5 59 57	July 9	5 59 12
July 20	6 01 33	6 00 45	5 59 59	July 19	5 59 14
July 30	6 01 35	6 00 47	6 00 01	July 29	5 59 16
Aug. 9	6 01 37	6 00 49	6 00 03	Aug. 8	5 59 18
Aug. 19	6 01 38	6 00 51	6 00 05	Aug. 18	5 59 20
Aug. 29	6 01 40	6 00 53	6 00 07	Aug. 28	5 59 22
Sept. 8	6 01 41	6 00 54	6 00 08	Sept. 7	5 59 23
Sept. 18	6 01 42	6 00 55	6 00 09	Sept. 17	5 59 24
Sept. 28	6 01 43	6 00 56	6 00 10	Sept. 27	5 59 25
Oct. 8	6 01 43	6 00 55	6 00 10	Oct. 7	5 59 25
Oct. 18	6 01 42	6 00 55	6 00 09	Oct. 17	5 59 24
Oct. 28	6 01 40	6 00 53	6 00 08	Oct. 27	5 59 23
Nov. 7	6 01 38	6 00 51	6 00 06	Nov. 6	5 59 21
Nov. 17	6 01 35	6 00 48	6 00 03	Nov. 16	5 59 18
Nov. 27	6 01 31	6 00 45	5 59 59	Nov. 26	5 59 14
Dec. 7	6 01 27	6 00 40	5 59 55	Dec. 6	5 59 10
Dec. 17	6 01 22	6 00 36	5 59 50	Dec. 16	5 59 05
Dec. 27	6 01 17	6 00 31	5 59 45	Dec. 26	5 59 00
Jan. 6	6 01 12	6 00 26	5 59 40	Jan. 5	5 58 55

SIDEREAL LONGITUDE OF THE VERNAL POINT

Referred to Spica as Fiducial

Date		1941	1942	1943	Date		1944
		° ′ ″	° ′ ″	° ′ ″			° ′ ″
Jan.	1	♓ 58 57	♓ 58 13	♓ 57 28	Jan.	1	♓ 56 43
Jan.	11	5 58 52	5 58 08	5 57 23	Jan.	11	5 56 37
Jan.	21	5 58 47	5 58 03	5 57 18	Jan.	21	5 56 32
Jan.	31	5 58 42	5 57 58	5 57 13	Jan.	31	5 56 27
Feb.	10	5 58 37	5 57 53	5 57 08	Feb.	10	5 56 22
Feb.	20	5 58 33	5 57 49	5 57 04	Feb.	20	5 56 18
Mar.	2	5 58 30	5 57 46	5 57 01	Mar.	1	5 56 15
Mar.	12	5 58 27	5 57 43	5 56 58	Mar.	11	5 56 12
Mar.	22	5 58 25	5 57 40	5 56 55	Mar.	21	5 56 09
Apr.	1	5 58 23	5 57 38	5 56 53	Mar.	31	5 56 07
Apr.	11	5 58 22	5 57 37	5 56 52	Apr.	10	5 56 06
Apr.	21	5 58 21	5 57 36	5 56 51	Apr.	20	5 56 05
May	1	5 58 21	5 57 36	5 56 51	Apr.	30	5 56 05
May	11	5 58 21	5 57 36	5 56 51	May	10	5 56 05
May	21	5 58 21	5 57 37	5 56 52	May	20	5 56 05
May	31	5 58 22	5 57 38	5 56 52	May	30	5 56 06
June	10	5 58 23	5 57 39	5 56 53	June	9	5 56 07
June	20	5 58 25	5 57 40	5 56 55	June	19	5 56 08
June	30	5 58 26	5 57 42	5 56 56	June	29	5 56 10
July	10	5 58 28	5 57 43	5 56 58	July	9	5 56 11
July	20	5 58 30	5 57 45	5 57 00	July	19	5 56 13
July	30	5 58 32	5 57 47	5 57 02	July	29	5 56 15
Aug.	9	5 58 34	5 57 49	5 57 04	Aug.	8	5 56 17
Aug.	19	5 58 36	5 57 51	5 57 06	Aug.	18	5 56 19
Aug.	29	5 58 37	5 57 53	5 57 07	Aug.	28	5 56 20
Sept.	8	5 58 39	5 57 54	5 57 09	Sept.	7	5 56 22
Sept.	18	5 58 40	5 57 55	5 57 10	Sept.	17	5 56 23
Sept.	28	5 58 41	5 57 56	5 57 10	Sept.	27	5 56 23
Oct.	8	5 58 41	5 57 56	5 57 10	Oct.	7	5 56 23
Oct.	18	5 58 40	5 57 55	5 57 10	Oct.	17	5 56 22
Oct.	28	5 58 38	5 57 54	5 57 08	Oct.	27	5 56 21
Nov.	7	5 58 36	5 57 52	5 57 06	Nov.	6	5 56 19
Nov.	17	5 58 33	5 57 49	5 57 03	Nov.	16	5 56 16
Nov.	27	5 58 30	5 57 45	5 56 59	Nov.	26	5 56 12
Dec.	7	5 58 25	5 57 41	5 56 55	Dec.	6	5 56 08
Dec.	17	5 58 20	5 57 36	5 56 50	Dec.	16	5 56 03
Dec.	27	5 58 15	5 57 31	5 56 45	Dec.	26	5 55 58
Jan.	6	5 58 10	5 57 26	5 56 40	Jan.	5	5 55 53

SIDEREAL LONGITUDE OF THE VERNAL POINT

Referred to Spica as Fiducial

Date		Common Years 1945	1946	1947	Leap Year 1948		
		° ′ ″	° ′ ″	° ′ ″			° ′ ″
Jan.	1	♓ 55 55	♓ 55 05	♓ 54 14	Jan.	1	♓ 53 21
Jan.	11	5 55 49	5 55 00	5 54 09	Jan.	11	5 53 16
Jan.	21	5 55 44	5 54 55	5 54 03	Jan.	21	5 53 10
Jan.	31	5 55 39	5 54 50	5 53 58	Jan.	31	5 53 05
Feb.	10	5 55 34	5 54 45	5 53 53	Feb.	10	5 53 00
Feb.	20	5 55 30	5 54 41	5 53 49	Feb.	20	5 52 56
Mar.	2	5 55 27	5 54 37	5 53 45	Mar.	1	5 52 52
Mar.	12	5 55 24	5 54 34	5 53 42	Mar.	11	5 52 49
Mar.	22	5 55 21	5 54 31	5 53 40	Mar.	21	5 52 46
Apr.	1	5 55 19	5 54 29	5 53 38	Mar.	31	5 52 44
Apr.	11	5 55 18	5 54 28	5 53 36	Apr.	10	5 52 43
Apr.	21	5 55 17	5 54 27	5 53 35	Apr.	20	5 52 42
May	1	5 55 17	5 54 27	5 53 35	Apr.	30	5 52 41
May	11	5 55 17	5 54 26	5 53 34	May	10	5 52 41
May	21	5 55 17	5 54 27	5 53 35	May	20	5 52 41
May	31	5 55 18	5 54 27	5 53 35	May	30	5 52 41
June	10	5 55 19	5 54 28	5 53 36	June	9	5 52 42
June	20	5 55 20	5 54 29	5 53 37	June	19	5 52 43
June	30	5 55 21	5 54 31	5 53 39	June	29	5 52 45
July	10	5 55 23	5 54 33	5 53 40	July	9	5 52 46
July	20	5 55 25	5 54 34	5 53 42	July	19	5 52 48
July	30	5 55 27	5 54 36	5 53 44	July	29	5 52 49
Aug.	9	5 55 29	5 54 38	5 53 45	Aug.	8	5 52 51
Aug.	19	5 55 30	5 54 40	5 53 47	Aug.	18	5 52 53
Aug.	29	5 55 32	5 54 41	5 53 49	Aug.	28	5 52 54
Sept.	8	5 55 33	5 54 42	5 53 50	Sept.	7	5 52 56
Sept.	18	5 55 34	5 54 43	5 53 51	Sept.	17	5 52 56
Sept.	28	5 55 34	5 54 44	5 53 51	Sept.	27	5 52 57
Oct.	8	5 55 34	5 54 43	5 53 51	Oct.	7	5 52 56
Oct.	18	5 55 33	5 54 42	5 53 50	Oct.	17	5 52 55
Oct.	28	5 55 32	5 54 41	5 53 48	Oct.	27	5 52 54
Nov.	7	5 55 30	5 54 38	5 53 46	Nov.	6	5 52 51
Nov.	17	5 55 27	5 54 35	5 53 43	Nov.	16	5 52 48
Nov.	27	5 55 23	5 54 31	5 53 39	Nov.	26	5 52 44
Dec.	7	5 55 18	5 54 27	5 53 34	Dec.	6	5 52 40
Dec.	17	5 55 13	5 54 22	5 53 29	Dec.	16	5 52 35
Dec.	27	5 55 08	5 54 17	5 53 24	Dec.	26	5 52 29
Jan.	6	5 55 03	5 54 12	5 53 19	Jan.	5	5 52 24

SIDEREAL LONGITUDE OF THE VERNAL POINT

Referred to Spica as Fiducial

Date	Common Years 1949	1950	1951	Leap Year 1952 Date	1952
	° ′ ″	° ′ ″	° ′ ″		° ′ ″
Jan. 1	♓ 52 26	♓ 51 31	♓ 50 35	Jan. 1	♓ 49 40
Jan. 11	5 52 21	5 51 25	5 50 30	Jan. 11	5 49 34
Jan. 21	5 52 15	5 51 20	5 50 24	Jan. 21	5 49 29
Jan. 31	5 52 10	5 51 15	5 50 19	Jan. 31	5 49 24
Feb. 10	5 52 05	5 51 10	5 50 14	Feb. 10	5 49 19
Feb. 20	5 52 01	5 51 05	5 50 10	Feb. 20	5 49 14
Mar. 2	5 51 57	5 51 02	5 50 06	Mar. 1	5 49 10
Mar. 12	5 51 54	5 50 58	5 50 03	Mar. 11	5 49 07
Mar. 22	5 51 51	5 50 56	5 50 00	Mar. 21	5 49 04
Apr. 1	5 51 49	5 50 54	5 49 58	Mar. 31	5 49 02
Apr. 11	5 51 48	5 50 52	5 49 56	Apr. 10	5 49 01
Apr. 21	5 51 47	5 50 51	5 49 55	Apr. 20	5 49 00
May 1	5 51 46	5 50 50	5 49 54	Apr. 30	5 48 59
May 11	5 51 46	5 50 50	5 49 54	May 10	5 48 59
May 21	5 51 46	5 50 50	5 49 54	May 20	5 48 59
May 31	5 51 46	5 50 51	5 49 55	May 30	5 48 59
June 10	5 51 47	5 50 52	5 49 56	June 9	5 49 00
June 20	5 51 48	5 50 53	5 49 57	June 19	5 49 01
June 30	5 51 50	5 50 54	5 49 58	June 29	5 49 02
July 10	5 51 51	5 50 55	5 49 59	July 9	5 49 04
July 20	5 51 53	5 50 57	5 50 01	July 19	5 49 05
July 30	5 51 55	5 50 59	5 50 03	July 29	5 49 07
Aug. 9	5 51 56	5 51 00	5 50 04	Aug. 8	5 49 09
Aug. 19	5 51 58	5 51 02	5 50 06	Aug. 18	5 49 10
Aug. 29	5 51 59	5 51 03	5 50 07	Aug. 28	5 49 12
Sept. 8	5 52 00	5 51 04	5 50 08	Sept. 7	5 49 13
Sept. 18	5 52 01	5 51 05	5 50 09	Sept. 17	5 49 14
Sept. 28	5 52 01	5 51 05	5 50 09	Sept. 27	5 49 14
Oct. 8	5 52 01	5 51 05	5 50 09	Oct. 7	5 49 14
Oct. 18	5 52 00	5 51 04	5 50 08	Oct. 17	5 49 13
Oct. 28	5 51 58	5 51 02	5 50 06	Oct. 27	5 49 11
Nov. 7	5 51 56	5 51 00	5 50 04	Nov. 6	5 49 09
Nov. 17	5 51 53	5 50 57	5 50 01	Nov. 16	5 49 06
Nov. 27	5 51 49	5 50 53	5 49 57	Nov. 26	5 49 02
Dec. 7	5 51 44	5 50 48	5 49 53	Dec. 6	5 48 58
Dec. 17	5 51 39	5 50 43	5 49 48	Dec. 16	5 48 53
Dec. 27	5 51 33	5 50 38	5 49 42	Dec. 26	5 48 48
Jan. 6	5 51 28	5 50 33	5 49 37	Jan. 5	5 48 42

SIDEREAL LONGITUDE OF THE VERNAL POINT

Referred to Spica as Fiducial

Date		1953	1954	1955	Leap Year		1956
		° ′ ″	° ′ ″	° ′ ″			° ′ ″
Jan.	1	♓ 48 44	♓ 47 51	♓ 47 00	Jan.	1	♓ 46 10
Jan.	11	5 48 39	5 47 46	5 46 54	Jan.	11	5 46 05
Jan.	21	5 48 33	5 47 40	5 46 49	Jan.	21	5 45 59
Jan.	31	5 48 28	5 47 35	5 46 44	Jan.	31	5 45 54
Feb.	10	5 48 23	5 47 30	5 46 39	Feb.	10	5 45 50
Feb.	20	5 48 19	5 47 26	5 46 35	Feb.	20	5 45 46
Mar.	2	5 48 15	5 47 22	5 46 31	Mar.	1	5 45 42
Mar.	12	5 48 12	5 47 19	5 46 28	Mar.	11	5 45 39
Mar.	22	5 48 10	5 47 17	5 46 25	Mar.	21	5 45 36
Apr.	1	5 48 08	5 47 15	5 46 23	Mar.	31	5 45 34
Apr.	11	5 48 06	5 47 13	5 46 22	Apr.	10	5 45 33
Apr.	21	5 48 05	5 47 12	5 46 21	Apr.	20	5 45 32
May	1	5 48 04	5 47 12	5 46 21	Apr.	30	5 45 32
May	11	5 48 04	5 47 11	5 46 21	May	10	5 45 32
May	21	5 48 04	5 47 12	5 46 21	May	20	5 45 32
May	31	5 48 05	5 47 12	5 46 21	May	30	5 45 33
June	10	5 48 06	5 47 13	5 46 22	June	9	5 45 34
June	20	5 48 07	5 47 14	5 46 23	June	19	5 45 35
June	30	5 48 08	5 47 16	5 46 25	June	29	5 45 36
July	10	5 48 10	5 47 17	5 46 27	July	9	5 45 38
July	20	5 48 11	5 47 19	5 46 28	July	19	5 45 40
July	30	5 48 13	5 47 21	5 46 30	July	29	5 45 42
Aug.	9	5 48 15	5 47 22	5 46 32	Aug.	8	5 45 44
Aug.	19	5 48 17	5 47 24	5 46 34	Aug.	18	5 45 45
Aug.	29	5 48 18	5 47 26	5 46 35	Aug.	28	5 45 47
Sept.	8	5 48 19	5 47 27	5 46 37	Sept.	7	5 45 48
Sept.	18	5 48 20	5 47 28	5 46 38	Sept.	17	5 45 49
Sept.	28	5 48 20	5 47 28	5 46 38	Sept.	27	5 45 50
Oct.	8	5 48 20	5 47 28	5 46 38	Oct.	7	5 45 50
Oct.	18	5 48 19	5 47 27	5 46 37	Oct.	17	5 45 49
Oct.	28	5 48 18	5 47 26	5 46 36	Oct.	27	5 45 48
Nov.	7	5 48 15	5 47 23	5 46 33	Nov.	6	5 45 46
Nov.	17	5 48 12	5 47 20	5 46 30	Nov.	16	5 45 43
Nov.	27	5 48 08	5 47 17	5 46 27	Nov.	26	5 45 39
Dec.	7	5 48 04	5 47 12	5 46 22	Dec.	6	5 45 35
Dec.	17	5 47 59	5 47 07	5 46 17	Dec.	16	5 45 30
Dec.	27	5 47 54	5 47 02	5 46 12	Dec.	26	5 45 25
Jan.	6	5 47 49	5 46 57	5 46 07	Jan.	5	5 45 20

SIDEREAL LONGITUDE OF THE VERNAL POINT

Referred to Spica as Fiducial

Date	Common Years 1957	1958	1959	Leap Year 1960	
	° ′ ″	° ′ ″	° ′ ″		° ′ ″
Jan. 1	♓ 45 22	♓ 44 36	♓ 43 51	Jan. 1	♓ 43 06
Jan. 11	5 45 17	5 44 30	5 43 45	Jan. 11	5 43 01
Jan. 21	5 45 11	5 44 25	5 43 40	Jan. 21	5 42 56
Jan. 31	5 45 06	5 44 20	5 43 35	Jan. 31	5 42 51
Feb. 10	5 45 02	5 44 16	5 43 31	Feb. 10	5 42 46
Feb. 20	5 44 58	5 44 12	5 43 27	Feb. 20	5 42 42
Mar. 2	5 44 54	5 44 08	5 43 23	Mar. 1	5 42 39
Mar. 12	5 44 51	5 44 05	5 43 20	Mar. 11	5 42 36
Mar. 22	5 44 49	5 44 03	5 43 18	Mar. 21	5 42 33
Apr. 1	5 44 47	5 44 01	5 43 16	Mar. 31	5 42 31
Apr. 11	5 44 46	5 44 00	5 43 15	Apr. 10	5 42 30
Apr. 21	5 44 45	5 43 59	5 43 14	Apr. 20	5 42 29
May 1	5 44 44	5 43 59	5 43 14	Apr. 30	5 42 29
May 11	5 44 44	5 43 59	5 43 14	May 10	5 42 29
May 21	5 44 45	5 43 59	5 43 14	May 20	5 42 30
May 31	5 44 46	5 44 00	5 43 15	May 30	5 42 31
June 10	5 44 47	5 44 01	5 43 16	June 9	5 42 32
June 20	5 44 48	5 44 02	5 43 17	June 19	5 42 33
June 30	5 44 49	5 44 04	5 43 19	June 29	5 42 34
July 10	5 44 51	5 44 05	5 43 21	July 9	5 42 36
July 20	5 44 53	5 44 07	5 43 23	July 19	5 42 38
July 30	5 44 55	5 44 09	5 43 24	July 29	5 42 40
Aug. 9	5 44 57	5 44 11	5 43 26	Aug. 8	5 42 42
Aug. 19	5 44 59	5 44 13	5 43 28	Aug. 18	5 42 44
Aug. 29	5 45 00	5 44 15	5 43 30	Aug. 28	5 42 46
Sept. 8	5 45 02	5 44 16	5 43 32	Sept. 7	5 42 47
Sept. 18	5 45 03	5 44 17	5 43 33	Sept. 17	5 42 48
Sept. 28	5 45 03	5 44 18	5 43 33	Sept. 27	5 42 49
Oct. 8	5 45 03	5 44 18	5 43 33	Oct. 7	5 42 49
Oct. 18	5 45 02	5 44 17	5 43 32	Oct. 17	5 42 48
Oct. 28	5 45 01	5 44 16	5 43 31	Oct. 27	5 42 47
Nov. 7	5 44 59	5 44 14	5 43 29	Nov. 6	5 42 45
Nov. 17	5 44 56	5 44 11	5 43 26	Nov. 16	5 42 42
Nov. 27	5 44 52	5 44 07	5 43 23	Nov. 26	5 42 38
Dec. 7	5 44 48	5 44 03	5 43 18	Dec. 6	5 42 34
Dec. 17	5 44 43	5 43 58	5 43 14	Dec. 16	5 42 30
Dec. 27	5 44 38	5 43 53	5 43 09	Dec. 26	5 42 25
Jan. 6	5 44 33	5 43 48	5 43 04	Jan. 5	5 42 20

HOW TO DETERMINE CAMPANIAN HOUSE CUSPS USING A STANDARD PLACIDIAN TABLES OF HOUSES

THERE ARE A NUMBER of convenient methods by which the student may determine the Campanian cusps for the "intermediate houses" through the use of the standard Placidian tables of houses in his possession. Such methods are familiar to many, since the issue of house-division has been treated at length in Alan Leo's works, and in excellent articles over the years which have appeared in various astrological journals. To improve upon these known methods, and to eliminate the need to resort to trigonometry and a long list of confusing rules, we present here simple directions and adequate tables which enable the student to find the desired Campanian cusps quickly.

The longitudes of the Midheaven and Ascendant are identical in both the Placidian and Campanian systems. For any given sidereal time and latitude, the student must enter his ordinary tables of houses and extract the culminating and rising degrees. If the chart he is computing is to be shown in terms of sidereal longitude, he may immediately apply the VP, thereby finding the sidereal longitudes of the First and Tenth cusps.

In the system we are outlining, once the chart-angles are treated properly in this way, the student need only use the Midheaven as found in order to obtain the Campanian cusps of the Eleventh, Twelfth, Second and Third houses. The procedure is merely to find in the four brief tables herewith the certain number of degrees one must add to the longitude of the Midheaven in order to find the longitudes on the cusps of the intermediate houses in question.

The four tables which follow are to be entered, using the sidereal time and the geographical latitude as arguments. The values in the body of each table show the number of degrees, and tenths of a degree, to be added directly to the Midheaven, for the appropriate house. The values are given to tenths of a degree to facilitate the accuracy of interpolating vertically and cross-wise, although the final answer, after simple addition, should be "rounded off" to the nearest whole degree. Students who know how to do "curvilinear interpolation" (which can easily be learned from Chamber's table and instructions headed, "Binomial Coefficients for Interpolation by Differences") need not round-off their answers, for they will be correct within a tenth of a degree.

For a beginner's example, let us assume the S. T. to be 17:20, and the latitude to be 45° North. The tropical longitude of the Midheaven, according to standard tables of houses, is therefore 20° 49′ of the sign Sagittarius. If the year is 1939, say, when the Vernal Point was 6° 00′ of Pisces, the sidereal longitude of the Midheaven is 26° 49′ of the constellation Scorpio. For all general purposes, this may be thought of simply as 26.8° Scorpio, or even just as 27° Scorpio. (The Ascendant should be taken out of the T. H. along with the Midheaven, and converted in the same way to its SZ equivalent. In the present instance, the TZ Ascendant is 11° 03' Pisces, which makes the SZ Ascendant 17° 03' Aquarius.)

The Campanian cusp of the Eleventh house is found by adding 11.7° to the Midheaven, which is 26.8° Scorpio. Hence, the Eleventh cusp in our example is 8.5° Sagittarius, which, when rounded off, is 9° Sagittarius.

The Campanian cusp of the Twelfth house is found by adding 30.2° to 26.8° Scorpio. Hence, the Twelfth cusp in our example is 27.0° Sagittarius, or simply 27° Sagittarius.

The Campanian cusp of the Second house is found by adding 143.9° to 26.8° Scorpio. Hence, the Second cusp in our example is 20.7° Aries, or, for all practical purposes, 21° Aries.

The Campanian cusp of the Third house is found by adding 167.4° to 26.8° Scorpio. Hence, the Third cusp in our example is 14.2° Taurus, or simply 14° Taurus.

After inspecting the tables thoroughly, with the foregoing example as a guide, the new student will have no difficulties in grasping the method and making regular use of it until complete Campanian tables of houses are available. (See page 128.)

AMOUNT TO BE ADDED TO MIDHEAVEN TO OBTAIN ELEVENTH CAMPANIAN HOUSE CUSP

Sidereal Time	\multicolumn{8}{c}{NORTH LATITUDE}
	25°	30°	35°	40°	45°	50°	55°	60°
h m	°	°	°	°	°	°	°	°
0 00	32.5	31.9	31.0	29.9	28.4	26.6	24.4	21.9
0 40	32.7	32.3	31.7	30.8	29.5	28.0	26.1	23.9
1 20	32.6	32.3	31.9	31.1	30.1	28.8	27.2	25.3
2 00	32.2	32.1	31.7	31.1	30.3	29.2	27.8	26.1
2 40	31.7	31.6	31.3	30.9	30.1	29.2	27.9	26.4
3 20	31.1	31.1	30.9	30.5	29.8	28.9	27.8	26.4
4 00	30.7	30.6	30.4	30.0	29.4	28.6	27.5	26.2
4 40	30.3	30.3	30.0	29.6	29.0	28.2	27.1	25.8
5 20	30.1	30.0	29.7	29.3	28.6	27.7	26.7	25.4
6 00	30.0	29.8	29.5	29.0	28.2	27.3	26.2	24.9
6 40	30.0	29.8	29.3	28.7	27.9	26.9	25.7	24.3
7 20	30.1	29.7	29.2	28.4	27.5	26.4	25.2	23.7
8 00	30.2	29.7	29.0	28.1	27.1	25.9	24.5	23.0
8 40	30.2	29.6	28.7	27.7	26.6	25.2	23.7	22.1
9 20	30.1	29.3	28.3	27.1	25.8	24.4	22.7	21.0
10 00	29.8	28.8	27.7	26.4	24.9	23.3	21.5	19.7
10 40	29.2	28.1	26.8	25.3	23.7	22.0	20.1	18.1
11 20	28.4	27.1	25.6	24.0	22.3	20.4	18.5	16.4
12 00	27.3	25.8	24.3	22.6	20.7	18.7	16.7	14.5
12 40	26.0	24.5	22.8	21.0	19.0	17.0	14.8	12.6
13 20	24.7	23.1	21.3	19.4	17.4	15.2	13.0	10.7
14 00	23.5	21.7	19.9	17.9	15.8	13.6	11.3	8.9
14 40	22.3	20.5	18.6	16.6	14.4	12.1	9.7	7.3
15 20	21.4	19.6	17.6	15.5	13.3	10.9	8.5	6.0
16 00	20.8	18.9	16.9	14.7	12.4	10.0	7.5	4.9
16 40	20.5	18.6	16.1	14.3	11.9	9.4	6.9	4.2
17 20	20.6	18.6	16.5	14.2	11.7	9.2	6.5	3.8
18 00	21.0	19.0	16.8	14.5	12.0	9.3	6.6	3.8
18 40	21.7	19.7	17.6	15.2	12.6	9.9	7.1	4.1
19 20	22.8	20.9	18.7	16.3	13.7	10.9	8.0	4.9
20 00	24.2	22.4	20.2	17.9	15.2	12.4	9.4	6.2
20 40	26.7	24.1	22.1	19.8	17.2	14.4	11.3	8.1
21 20	27.6	26.1	24.2	22.0	19.5	16.8	13.7	10.4
22 00	29.3	28.0	26.3	24.3	22.1	19.4	16.5	13.2
22 40	30.8	29.7	28.3	26.6	24.5	22.1	19.4	16.3
23 20	31.9	31.0	29.9	28.5	26.7	24.6	22.1	19.3
24 00	32.5	31.9	31.0	29.9	28.4	26.6	24.4	21.9

AMOUNT TO BE ADDED TO MIDHEAVEN TO OBTAIN TWELFTH CAMPANIAN HOUSE CUSP

Sidereal Time	\multicolumn{9}{c}{NORTH LATITUDE}
	25°	30°	35°	40°	45°	50°	55°	60°
h m	°	°	°	°	°	°	°	°
0 00	68.3	69.1	69.8	70.3	70.7	70.7	70.4	69.7
0 40	67.2	68.2	68.9	69.6	70.0	70.3	70.2	69.8
1 20	65.9	66.8	67.6	68.3	68.0	69.0	69.0	68.7
2 00	64.5	65.4	66.1	66.7	67.1	67.3	67.2	66.9
2 40	63.1	63.9	64.6	65.0	65.3	65.4	65.2	64.8
3 20	62.0	62.7	63.2	63.5	63.6	63.5	63.2	62.5
4 00	61.1	61.6	62.0	62.1	62.0	61.8	61.2	60.8
4 40	60.5	60.8	61.0	60.9	60.6	60.1	59.3	58.3
5 20	60.1	60.2	60.1	59.8	59.3	58.6	57.6	56.3
6 00	60.0	59.8	59.5	58.9	58.2	57.2	55.9	54.3
6 40	60.0	59.5	58.9	58.1	57.1	55.8	54.2	52.3
7 20	59.9	59.2	58.3	57.2	55.9	54.3	52.5	50.3
8 00	59.8	58.8	57.6	56.2	54.4	52.7	50.6	48.1
8 40	59.4	58.1	56.6	55.0	53.1	50.9	48.5	45.8
9 20	58.7	57.1	55.4	53.4	51.2	48.8	46.1	43.1
10 00	57.6	55.8	53.8	51.6	49.1	46.4	43.4	40.1
10 40	56.2	54.1	51.9	49.4	46.7	43.7	40.4	36.9
11 20	54.4	52.1	49.6	46.9	44.0	40.7	37.2	33.4
12 00	52.4	49.9	47.2	44.3	41.1	37.6	33.8	29.8
12 40	50.3	47.7	44.8	41.6	38.2	34.5	30.4	26.1
13 20	48.4	45.6	42.5	39.2	35.5	31.5	27.2	22.6
14 00	46.7	43.8	40.5	37.0	33.1	28.8	24.2	19.3
14 40	45.4	42.2	39.0	35.2	31.1	26.6	21.7	16.4
15 20	44.7	41.6	37.2	34.1	29.7	24.8	19.6	14.0
16 00	44.7	41.4	37.8	33.6	29.0	23.8	18.2	11.6
16 40	45.4	42.1	38.3	34.0	29.1	23.6	17.5	10.9
17 20	46.8	43.6	39.8	35.3	30.2	24.3	17.7	10.5
18 00	49.0	45.9	42.2	37.8	32.5	26.3	19.1	11.2
18 40	51.9	49.1	45.6	41.3	36.1	29.7	22.0	13.3
19 20	55.2	52.9	49.8	46.0	41.0	34.7	26.8	17.3
20 00	58.8	57.0	54.6	51.4	47.1	41.3	33.7	23.9
20 40	62.3	61.1	59.4	57.0	53.7	49.0	42.4	33.2
21 20	65.2	64.6	63.7	62.2	59.9	56.6	51.7	44.4
22 00	67.3	67.3	67.0	66.2	65.0	63.0	59.9	55.0
22 40	68.5	68.9	69.0	68.9	68.5	67.5	65.8	62.9
23 20	68.7	69.4	69.9	70.2	70.3	70.0	69.2	67.7
24 00	68.3	69.1	69.8	70.3	70.7	70.7	70.4	69.7

AMOUNT TO BE ADDED TO MIDHEAVEN TO OBTAIN SECOND CAMPANIAN HOUSE CUSP

Sidereal Time	\multicolumn{8}{c}{NORTH LATITUDE}
h m	25°	30°	35°	40°	45°	50°	55°	60°
0 00	127.6	130.1	132.8	135.7	138.9	142.4	146.2	150.2
0 40	125.6	127.9	130.4	133.1	136.0	139.3	142.8	146.6
1 20	123.8	125.9	128.1	130.6	133.3	136.3	139.6	143.1
2 00	122.4	124.2	126.2	128.4	130.9	133.6	136.6	139.9
2 40	121.3	122.9	124.6	126.6	128.8	131.2	133.9	136.9
3 20	120.6	121.9	123.4	125.0	126.9	129.1	131.5	134.2
4 00	120.2	121.2	122.4	123.8	125.6	127.3	129.4	131.9
4 40	120.1	120.8	121.7	122.8	124.1	125.7	127.5	129.7
5 20	120.0	120.5	121.1	121.9	122.9	124.2	125.8	127.7
6 00	120.0	120.2	120.5	121.1	121.8	122.8	124.1	125.7
6 40	119.9	119.8	119.9	120.2	120.7	121.4	122.4	123.7
7 20	119.5	119.2	119.0	119.1	119.4	119.9	120.7	121.7
8 00	118.9	118.4	118.0	117.9	118.0	118.2	118.7	119.2
8 40	118.0	117.3	116.8	116.5	116.4	116.5	116.8	117.5
9 20	116.9	116.1	115.4	115.0	114.7	114.6	114.8	115.2
10 00	115.5	114.6	113.9	113.3	112.9	112.7	112.8	113.1
10 40	114.1	113.2	112.4	111.7	112.0	111.0	111.0	111.3
11 20	112.8	111.8	111.1	110.4	110.0	109.7	109.8	110.2
12 00	111.7	110.9	110.2	109.7	109.3	109.3	109.6	110.3
12 40	111.3	110.6	110.1	109.8	109.7	110.0	110.8	112.3
13 20	111.5	111.1	111.0	111.1	111.5	112.5	114.2	117.1
14 00	112.7	112.7	113.0	113.8	115.0	117.0	120.1	125.0
14 40	114.8	115.4	116.3	117.8	120.1	123.4	128.3	135.6
15 20	117.7	118.9	120.6	123.0	126.3	131.0	137.6	146.8
16 00	121.2	123.0	125.4	128.6	132.9	138.7	146.3	156.1
16 40	124.8	127.1	130.2	134.0	139.0	145.3	153.2	162.7
17 20	128.1	130.9	134.4	138.7	143.9	150.3	158.0	166.7
18 00	131.0	134.1	137.8	142.2	147.5	153.7	160.9	168.8
18 40	133.2	136.4	140.2	144.7	149.8	155.7	162.3	169.5
19 20	134.6	137.9	141.7	146.0	150.9	156.4	162.5	169.1
20 00	135.3	138.6	142.2	146.4	151.0	156.2	161.8	168.4
20 40	135.3	138.4	142.8	145.9	150.3	155.2	160.4	166.0
21 20	134.6	137.8	141.0	144.8	148.9	153.4	158.3	163.6
22 00	133.3	136.2	139.5	143.0	146.9	151.2	155.8	160.7
22 40	131.6	134.4	137.5	140.8	144.5	148.5	152.8	157.4
23 20	129.7	132.3	135.2	138.4	141.8	145.5	149.6	153.9
24 00	127.6	130.1	132.8	135.7	138.9	142.4	146.2	150.2

AMOUNT TO BE ADDED TO MIDHEAVEN TO OBTAIN THIRD CAMPANIAN HOUSE CUSP

Sidereal Time h m	\multicolumn{8}{c}{NORTH LATITUDE}							
	25°	30°	35°	40°	45°	50°	55°	60°
0 00	152.7	154.2	155.7	157.4	159.3	161.3	163.3	165.5
0 40	151.6	152.9	154.4	156.0	157.7	159.6	161.5	163.6
1 20	150.8	151.9	153.2	154.7	156.3	158.0	159.9	161.9
2 00	150.2	151.2	152.3	153.6	155.1	156.7	158.5	160.3
2 40	149.9	150.7	151.7	152.9	154.2	155.6	157.3	159.0
3 20	149.8	150.4	151.3	152.3	153.4	154.8	156.3	157.9
4 00	149.8	150.3	151.0	151.9	152.9	154.1	155.5	157.0
4 40	149.9	150.3	150.8	151.6	152.5	153.6	154.8	156.3
5 20	150.0	150.2	150.7	151.3	152.1	153.1	154.3	155.7
6 00	150.0	150.2	150.5	151.0	151.8	152.7	153.8	155.1
6 40	149.9	150.0	150.3	150.7	151.4	152.3	153.3	154.6
7 20	149.7	149.7	150.0	150.4	151.0	151.8	152.9	154.2
8 00	149.3	149.4	149.6	150.0	150.6	151.4	152.5	153.8
8 40	148.9	148.9	149.1	149.5	150.2	151.1	152.2	153.6
9 20	148.3	148.4	148.7	149.1	149.9	150.8	152.1	153.6
10 00	147.8	147.9	148.3	148.9	149.7	150.8	152.2	153.9
10 40	147.4	147.7	148.1	148.9	149.9	151.2	152.8	154.7
11 20	147.3	147.7	148.3	149.2	150.5	152.0	153.9	156.1
12 00	147.5	148.1	149.0	150.1	151.6	153.4	155.6	158.1
12 40	148.1	149.0	150.1	151.5	153.3	155.4	157.9	160.7
13 20	149.2	150.3	151.7	153.4	155.5	157.9	160.6	163.7
14 00	150.7	152.0	153.7	155.7	157.9	160.6	163.5	166.8
14 40	152.4	153.9	155.8	158.0	160.5	163.2	166.3	169.6
15 20	153.3	155.9	157.9	160.2	162.8	165.6	168.7	171.9
16 00	155.6	157.6	159.8	162.1	164.8	167.6	170.6	173.8
16 40	157.2	159.1	161.3	163.7	166.3	169.1	172.0	175.1
17 20	158.3	160.3	162.4	164.8	167.4	170.1	172.9	175.9
18 00	159.0	161.0	163.2	165.5	168.0	170.7	173.4	176.2
18 40	159.4	161.4	163.5	165.8	168.3	170.8	173.5	176.2
19 20	159.5	161.4	163.9	165.7	168.1	170.6	173.1	175.8
20 00	159.2	161.1	163.1	165.3	167.6	170.0	172.5	175.1
20 40	158.6	160.4	162.4	164.5	166.7	169.1	171.5	174.0
21 20	157.7	159.5	161.4	163.4	165.6	167.9	170.3	172.7
22 00	156.5	158.3	160.1	162.1	164.2	166.4	168.7	171.1
22 40	155.3	156.9	158.7	160.6	162.6	164.8	167.0	169.3
23 20	154.0	155.5	157.2	159.0	161.0	163.0	165.2	167.4
24 00	152.7	154.2	155.7	157.4	159.3	161.3	163.3	165.5

— 121 —

SOLAR AND LUNAR RETURNS

—— Illustrations ——

Figure 1: Radix of Sigmund Freud, Tropical Zodiac Version . 25
Figure 2: Radix of Sigmund Freud, Sidereal Zodiac Version . 25
Figure 3: Freud's Solar Return Preceding Demise . . . 25
Figure 4: Freud's Lunar Return Preceding Demise . . . 25
Figure 5: Lunar Return of "Self-Discovery" 58
Figure 6: Lunar Return of a Medical Fraud 59
Figure 7: Lunar Return of Discharge from Job 60
Figure 8: Lunar Return of Sudden Marriage 60
Figure 9: Lunar Return for Death of Warren G. Harding . 61
Figure 10: Lunar Return Preceding Presidential Oath of Calvin Coolidge 61
Figure 11: Nativity of Child Killed by Fire in Home . . . 63
Figure 12: Nativity of Child Equated to Locality of Death . 63
Figure 13: Solar Return of Child Preceding Death by Fire . 63
Figure 14: Lunar Return of Child Preceding Death by Fire . 63
Figure 15: Landru's Lunar Return Preceding Death Sentence . 66
Figure 16: Jack Dempsey's Solar Return Preceding Win of World Championship Title 68
Figure 17: Jack Dempsey's Lunar Return Preceding Win of World Championship Title 68
Figure 18: Jack Dempsey's Solar Return Preceding Loss of Title, 68
Figure 19: Jack Dempsey's Lunar Return Preceding Loss of Title 68
Figure 20: Lunar Return of Elizabeth Aldrich Preceding Demise 72
Figure 21: Lunar Return (Male) Preceding Arrest . . . 74

(See next page.)

HOW THEY AFFECT YOU
Illustrations — Continued

Figure 22: Nativity of William Heirens (alias George Murmans), 75
Figure 23: Heiren's Solar Return Preceding First Murder . 75
Figure 24: Natus of Thomas J. Mooney 79
Figure 25: Locus of Thomas J. Mooney 79
Figure 26: Lunar Return of Mooney Preceding Preparedness Day Bombing 79
Figure 27: Lunar Return of Mooney Preceding Full Pardon . 79
Figure 28: King Edward's Solar Return Preceding Abdication . 80
Figure 29: Edward's Lunar Return Preceding Abdication . 80
Figure 30: Last Solar Return for Leon Trotsky 81
Figure 31: Last Lunar Return for Leon Trotsky 81

ASTROLOGICAL ORIGINS
by Cyril Fagan

How has Astrology changed
through the centuries?
Where did it all begin?
Who cast the first horoscope?
What is the Sidereal Zodiac?

These questions are all answered in Cyril Fagan's amazing book *Astrological Origins.* In this revolutionary work, Cyril Fagan delves into the very beginnings of Astrology and comes up with some startling conclusions. Astrologers are using the wrong Zodiac! The Tropical Zodiac in common use today is now 24 degrees off from the true Sidereal Zodiac. Just how this error came about and what steps must be taken to rectify our Horoscopes, are thoroughly explained and documented in *Astrological Origins,* a new book from Llewellyn.

Cyril Fagan tells how the need to predict the rising of the Nile accounted for the naming of the constellations and how their simple names and symbols became invested with mysterious and occult meanings. The beginnings of the Hindu Zodiac are also explored, as is the role of Alexandre the Great in changing Hindu Astrology from the Tropical to the Sidereal. Cyril Fagan clears up much of the mystery surrounding Astrology and restores its original accuracy.

Read about the world's most ancient  Horoscope erected for the beginning of an era on July 16, 2767 BC. Star maps such as this were engraved in the pyramids and are used today to date important historical events. Learn how modern scholars used Astrology to find the true birthdate of Jesus Christ at the time of a Saturn-Jupiter conjunction in Pisces, in 7 BC. Many other biblical events can be accurately dated by using the Sidereal, rather than the Tropical Zodiac. By reviving this ancient astrological system Cyril Fagan has performed an outstanding service to Astrology. After this exciting discovery, Cyril Fagan will always be remembered as the "Father of Sidereal Astrology."

Paper, $2.95

Llewellyn Publications
Box 3383
St. Paul, Minn. 55165

ASTROLOGICAL BOOKS FOR STUDENTS

Llewellyn Publications is the oldest and largest publisher of Astrological and Occult books in the United States. We also maintain a complete stock of every book currently available in the English language on these subjects. Write for our catalogs. Your dealer will be happy to order any title you wish from us.

Llewellyn Publications
Box 3383
St. Paul, Minn. 55165